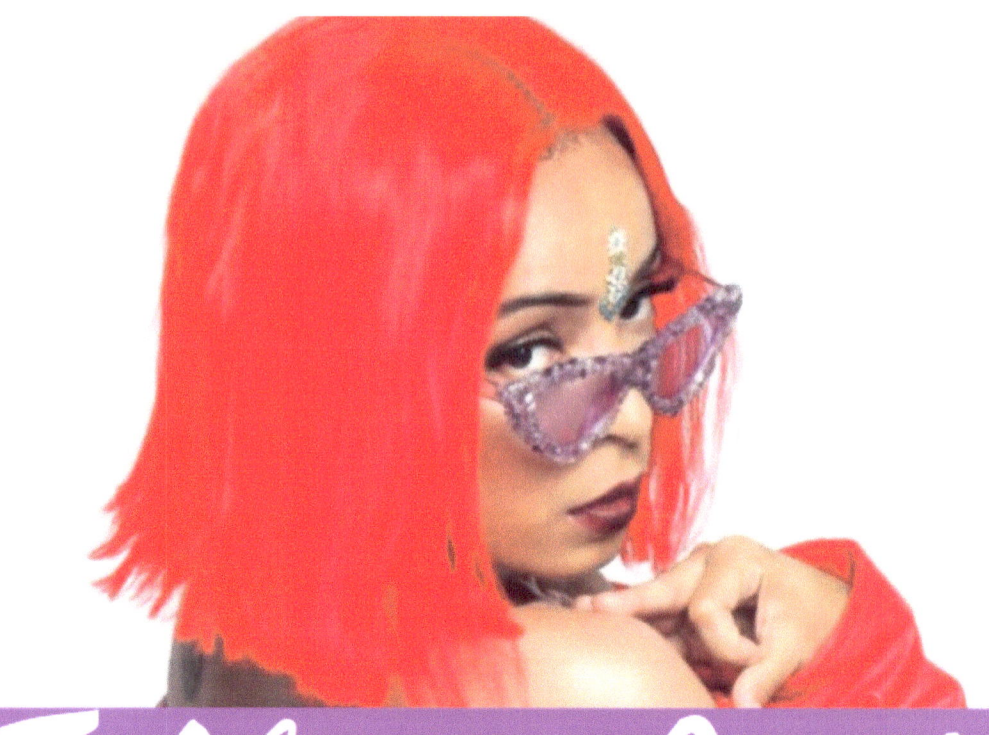

Table of Contents

⊕ **LETTER FROM THE EDITOR**

BETTER, FASTER, AND STRONGER

By Pilar Scratch

THE WORD THAT PARTICULARLY DRIVES ME WHEN THINKING F THIS ISSUE , STRENGTH . IN THIS ISSUE CONVEYS STRENGTH ANS PERSISTENCE . IN WHICH BOTH ELEMENTS ARE ESSENTIAL WHEN CONVERTING INTO AN ENTREPRENEUR .

Each issue we in fact become better , faster and stronger . It is vital to grow throughout time . Elevation is a key component in obtaining success . As we just completed our 4th yearly anniversary I am so proud of Fashion Gxd Magazine . We were just honored the prosperity award presented by prosperity nation , I Heart Radio and Power 105.1 . Growth.

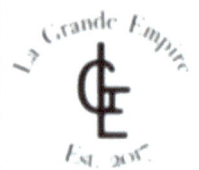

LA GRANDE EMPIRE

La Grande Empire is an apparel brand that is all about the style and essence of originality. We want our Emperors and Empresses to embrace their individuality and let their light shine while exuding confidence.

NETWORK! There is nothing more valuable than having face to face interactions with potential partners, mentors, customers, people that can make introductions, etc. People naturally go off of the vibe they receive to determine if they're going to buy from you or assist in your success. Remember customers buy from people, not the brand alone.

CONSISTENCY. Everyday is not going to be the best as an entrepreneur. There will be many of obstacles and rollercoaster events that may cause one to question oneself and ones abilities. Never give up and continue to make strides forward. Break through the barriers.

PATIENCE. Success in fashion is a jog not a sprint. Longevity is the goal here. You don't want to be a "one hit wonder" clothing line so to speak. You'll have the desire to get every design idea and new item out all at once but that is not productive.

BE OPEN TO CONSTRUCTIVE CRITICISM. Your team, no matter how small or large, were selected because you trust them and their abilities. Always be open to their feedback whether it is something you want to hear or not. They're looking from the outside in and have access to specific perspective(s) vs everything all at once. Allow their insights to make an impression on your thoughts and creativity.

TRUST THE PROCESS. What is destined, will eventually deliver.

website: www.lagrandeempire.com

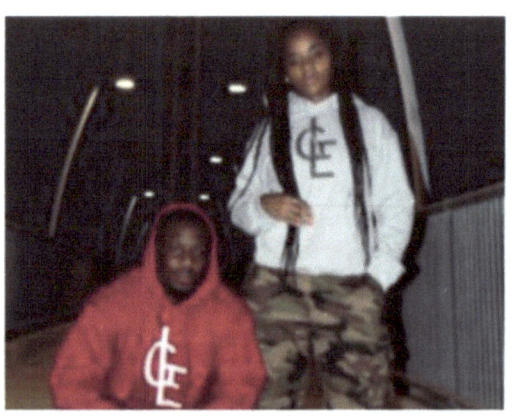

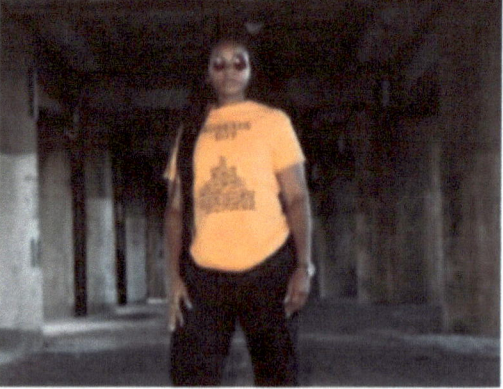

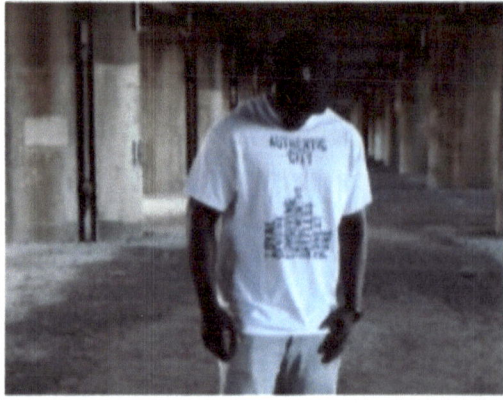

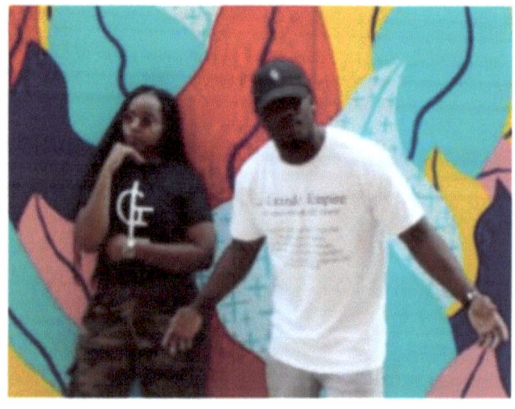

LIVING IN MY MIND

IFUEKO IGBINOVIA

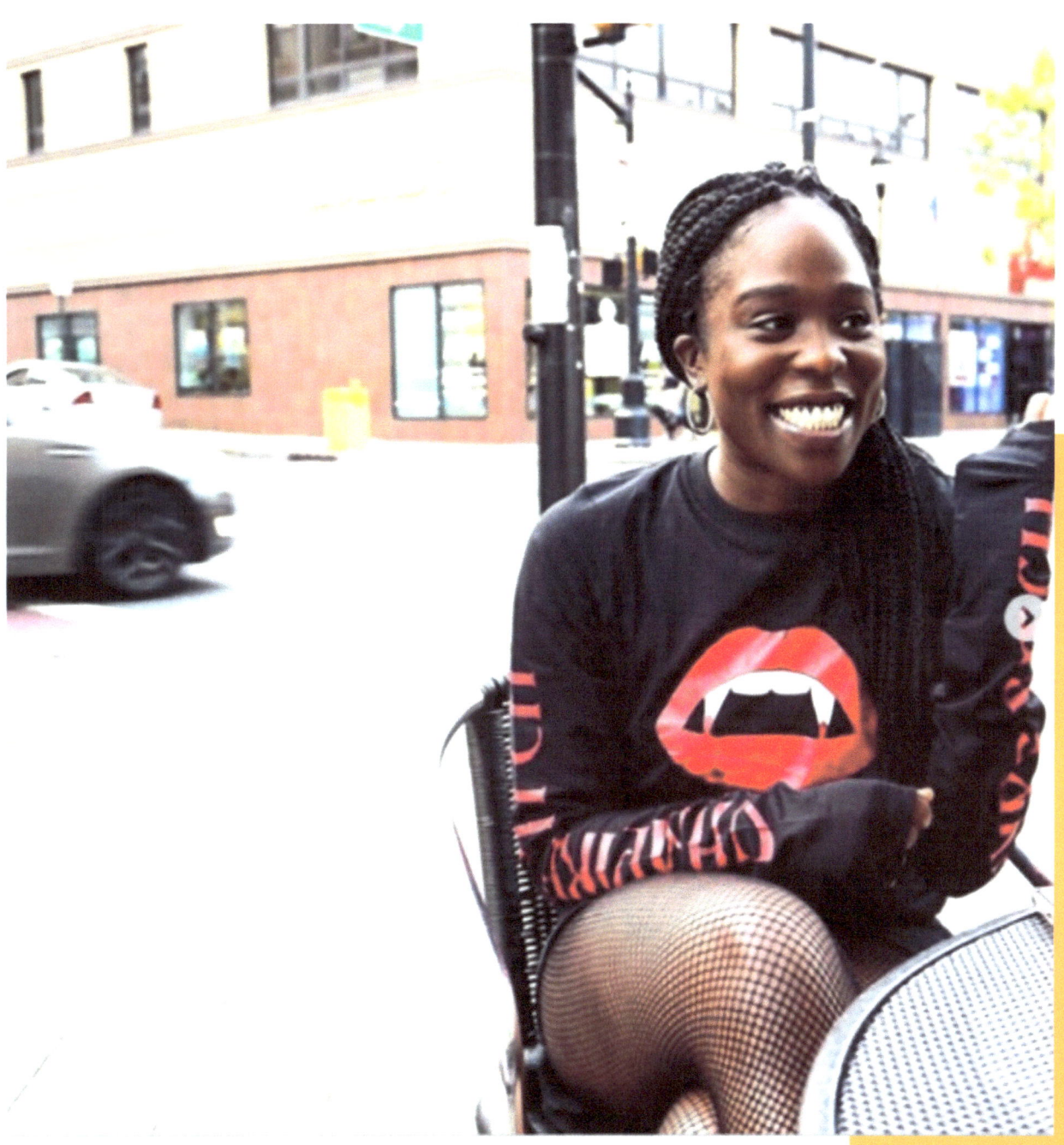

IFUEKO IGBINOVIA IS LIVING IN HER MIND ONE VIDEO AT A TIME
YOUTUBE.COM/LIVINGINMYMIND

NETER GOLD

FEATURING: A FEW TIPS ON STAYING YOURSELF & YOUR BUSINESS IN THIS PHOTOSHOPPED WORLD:

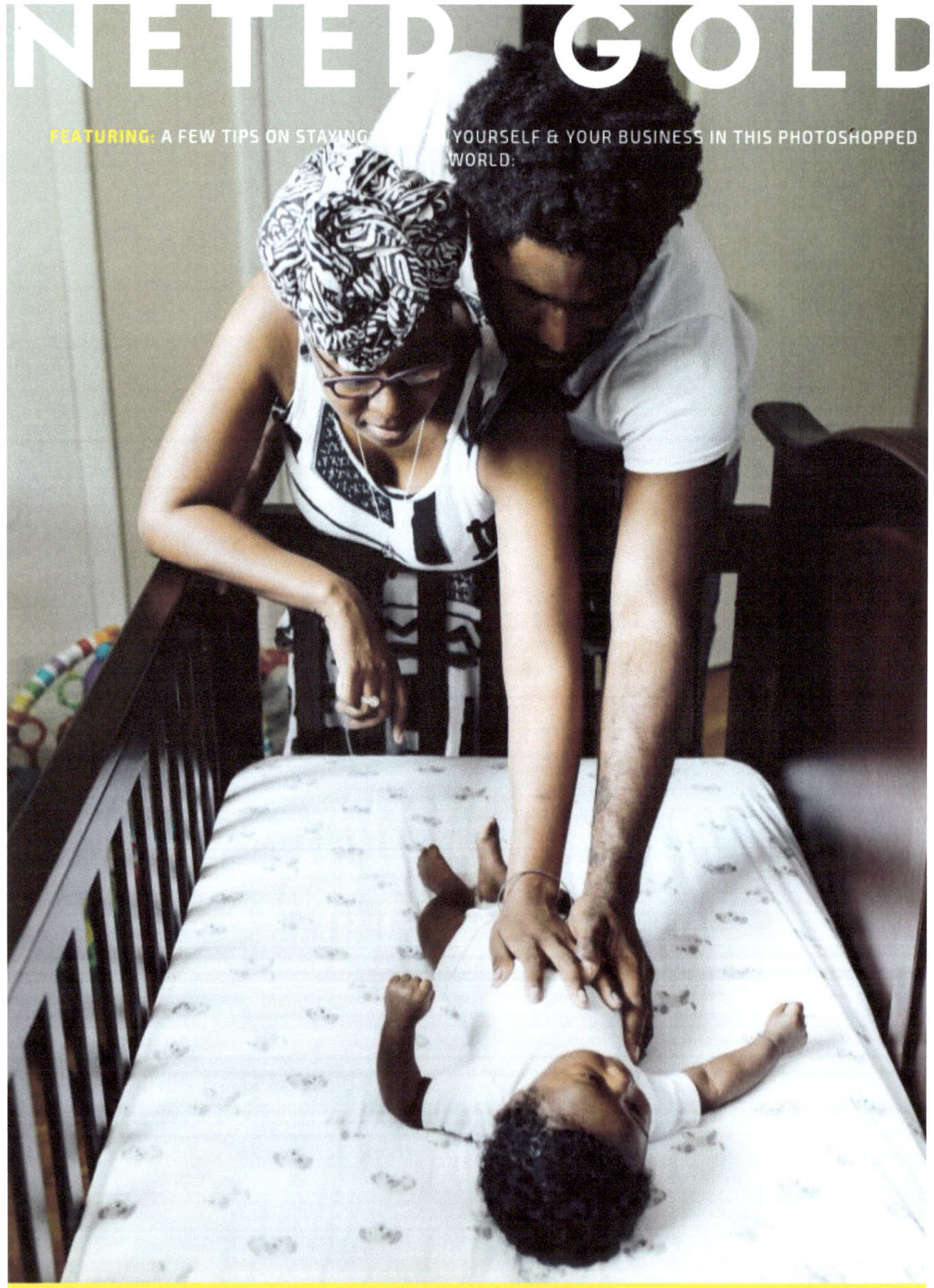

ISSUE NO. 17

PHOTO BY : ANGELA VAUGHN

A FEW TIPS ON STAYING TRUE TO YOURSELF & YOUR BUSINESS IN THIS PHOTOSHOPPED WORLD

WRITTEN ARTHUR CLEMENS

Neter Gold is a premiere all natural body care brand that has been making its name in the social media world by offering the world first and only oil infused wooded comb. To accompany their unique wooden hair tools they've also made it their business to donate 10% of their proceeds to four Washington, DC based non-profits..

1. Never forget your reason WHY.

When you started your business you had a solid reason why you wanted to start. Hopefully you haven't forgotten that WHY; it'll be the driving force when you are feeling down.

2. Always remember the WHO.

As your business grows so will your reach and the people you meet. Take time to reflect and pay appreciation to those who were there for you before everyone else was there for you.

3. WHEN the time is right don't be afraid.

There will be a moment in time when your next business decision will literally leave your heart pounding and your head turning; don't be afraid, go for it. The scariest decisions are often the ones you never believed you could achieve and are exactly the ones you should chase!

SOCIAL MEDIA

Facebook, Instagram, Twitter, & YouTube = Netergold

Website:
WWW.NTRGLD.COM

Effortless

BUILDING THE FUNDATION

What's the one thing that takes no effort whatsoever? The answer is being yourself. Effortless is built on a foundation for creative minds. Our team wants to inspire you to see anything's possible through determination & practice. We want you to strive to make what you love effortless by making it apart of who you are. The world needs creative individuals such as yourself to push us in the direction of the future. At the end of the day, this is your one and only life. Stay true to your roots and leave your mark on this world. When you're facing obstacles and feel like giving up.

Instagram: @effortlessOfficial
Website: www.Effortless.store
#RememberWhyYouDidIt

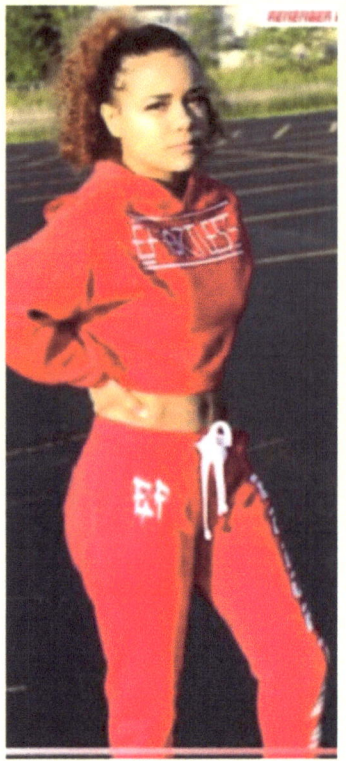
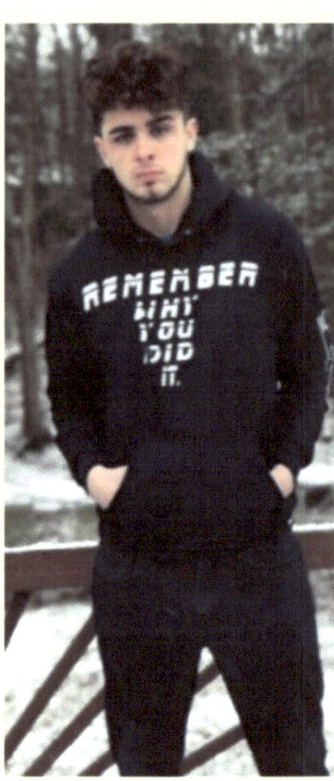

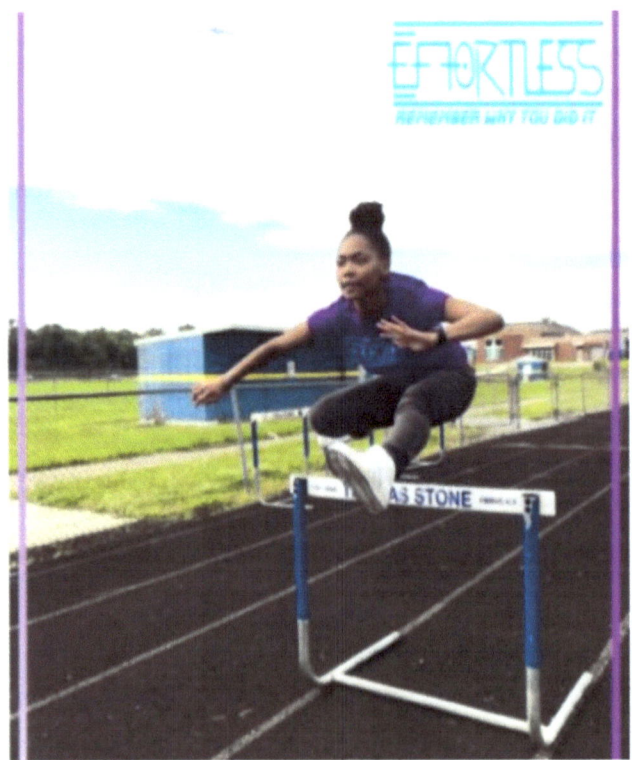

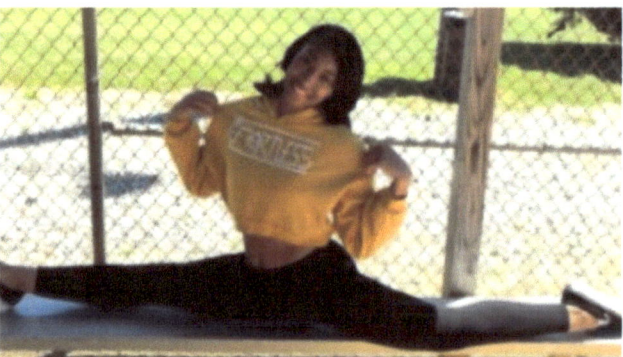

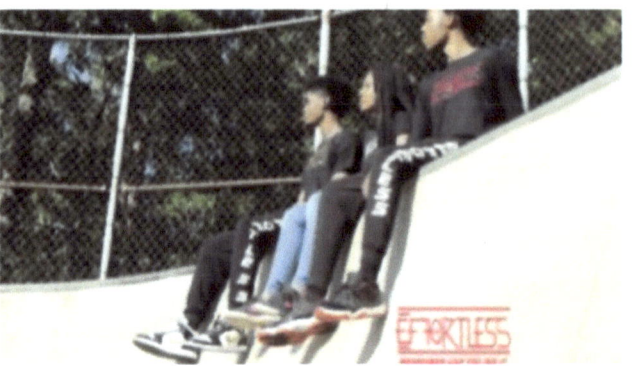

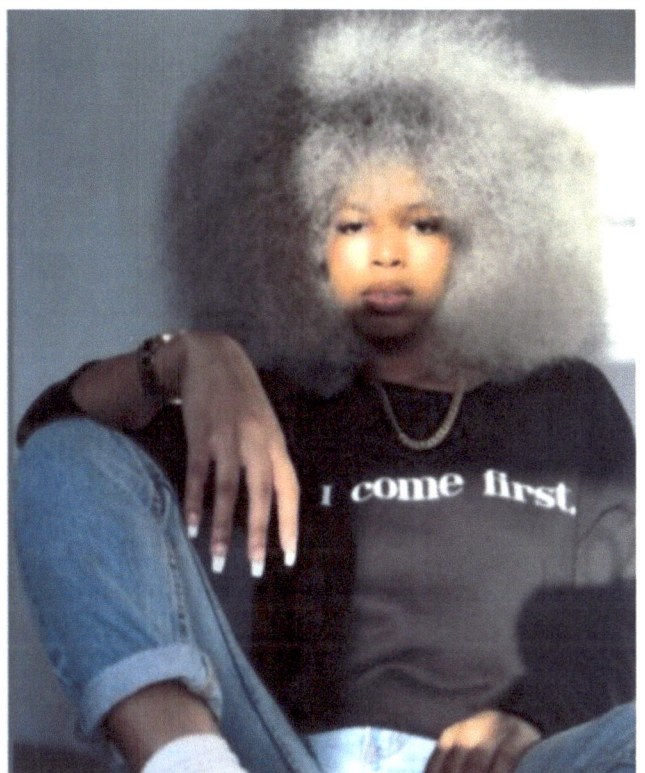

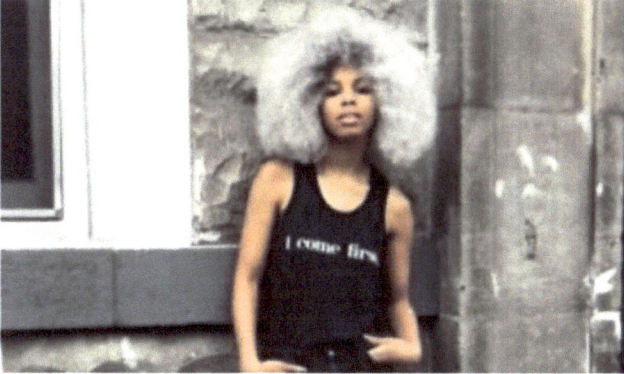

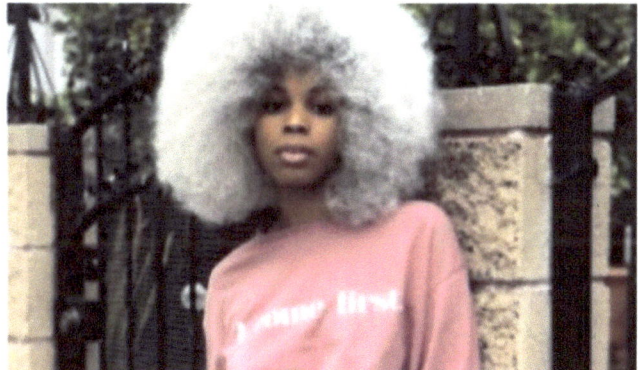

FIVE WAYS TO INVEST IN YOURSELF AS AN ENTREPRENEUR

Our only goal as beings is worth more than anything else, our unique life experiences make us the beautiful individuals that we are. Inspirational Affirmation Apparel is passionate about helping the people going through obstacles we believe and benefit through inspirational affirmations branded on you to remind yourselves that you are a force and you won't forget it ever again !

Inspirational Affirmation Apparel is an online clothing brand, established in 2014 by Allister and Denise Hill in Los Angeles, CA.

Make sure you always take care of yourself and mentally

Self care is monumental. It'll keep you motivated and on fire at all times. If you need a pause, just pause, but keep up with the work. Set yourself up for success by working more than anyone, wake up before they do, and go to sleep after them. That's the secret so many successful people talk about, just like Gary Vaynerchuck says, " You still have time from 7pm to 2am to work on your dreams and create something" Nothing is easy and it takes time so if you're not in a good mental state nothing will work, protect your energy, that's your number one asset.

Surround yourself with successful and hungry people

"Show me your friends and I'll tell you who you are", is more true than you can imagine. If your circle is filled with people that are not motivated, you're not going to be motivated. Multiple successful businessman and entrepreneurs shared this secret like Jason Capital, Grant Cardone, and Tai Lopez to name a few. See what you can change in your relationships to actually be around people that are going to push you and show you the way. Dan "The 50 Billion Dollar Man" Peña once said, "If you hang out with 4 millionaires, you're going to become the 5th one". Find yourself a mentor.

Do not be afraid to take risk

If it scares you, do it. We're meant to fight our fears and that's the source of extreme confidence and success. Everyone is scared of something, even your idols! The truth is they've became your idols because they fought through their fears. Go all the way in, head first. Successful entrepreneurs were not afraid to go broke or homeless for their message to be heard or their product to be used. That's just plain truth. Successful people love failure, because they always learn new things from it that make them so much stronger. Successful people love problems, because they can solve them. Don't be afraid to take risks, look out for them!

Become your biggest fan

Self confidence will change everything. Believe in yourself more than you believe in anything or anyone. It will make you a better seller to close people on your ideas and your dreams. Like we've said in the previous tip, fight your fears and it'll give you instant confidence. You'll feel like you're so much better than you were before you did it (and that's so important for your success). As humans we get most of our confidence from knowledge. The more you know, the more you'll feel safe and knowledgeable. Read books, the right ones. Email us at info@inspirationalaffirmationapparel.com to know which ones are worth reading to change your life ! Do not wait, the time is now !

Promote yourself

The one that will sell the most is not the best product, but the best known. Be omnipresent, be everywhere, all the time. Be so present that getting hated is inevitable. How could you do it, you ask? The answer is simple : Social media! Facebook, Instagram, Twitter, Pinterest, Youtube and so on. Put yourself out there, create your community and cherish them, talk to them, answer them and keep posting. Teach people stuff in your niche, show them how you do it, share anything and everything. Sorry to break it to you, but without giving a MASSIVE amount of value, no one will care about what you have to offer. Give first without asking for anything back, and know when to ask for it later. Obscurity is your biggest enemy. Get in the light, you can do it!

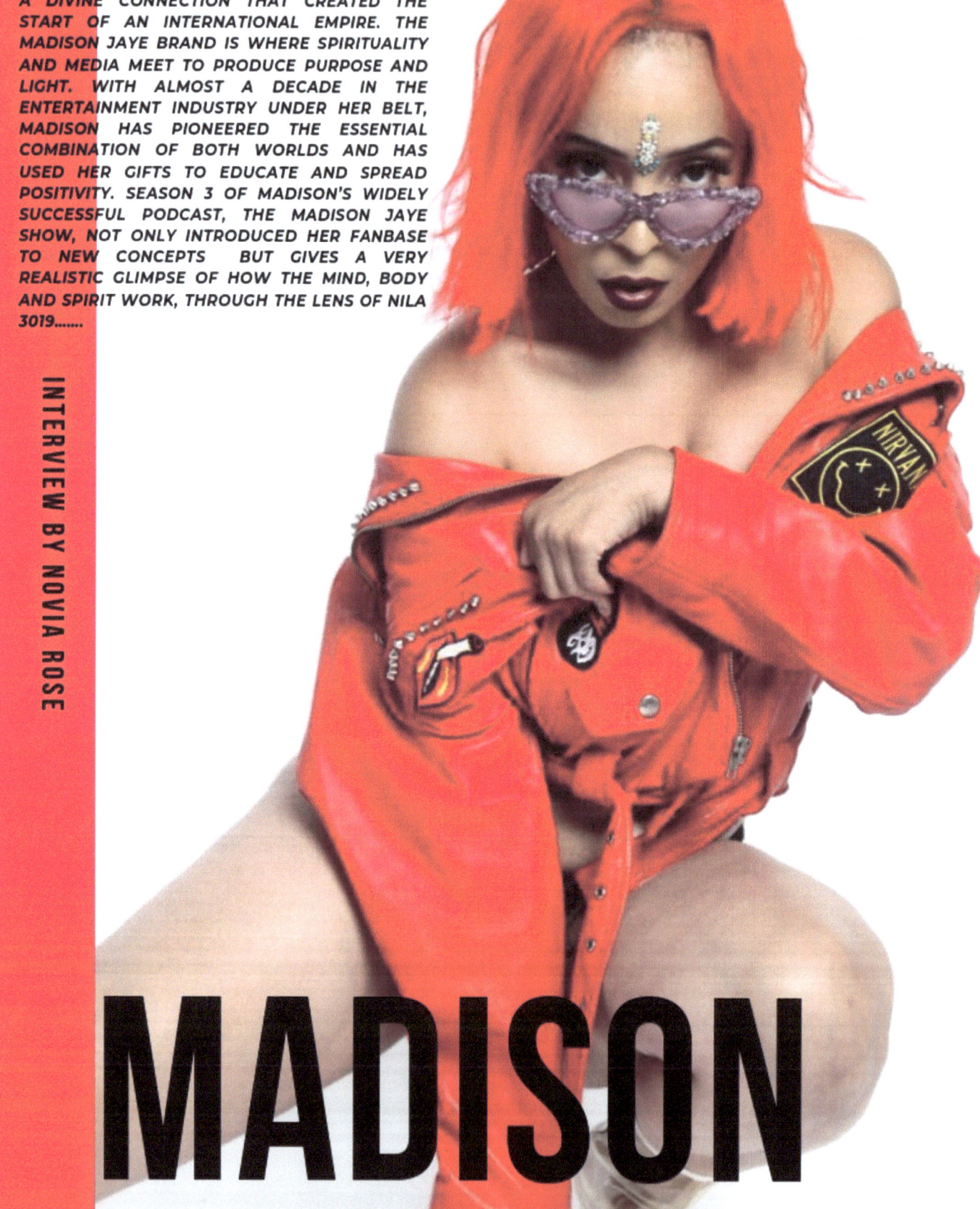

A DIVINE CONNECTION THAT CREATED THE START OF AN INTERNATIONAL EMPIRE. THE MADISON JAYE BRAND IS WHERE SPIRITUALITY AND MEDIA MEET TO PRODUCE PURPOSE AND LIGHT. WITH ALMOST A DECADE IN THE ENTERTAINMENT INDUSTRY UNDER HER BELT, MADISON HAS PIONEERED THE ESSENTIAL COMBINATION OF BOTH WORLDS AND HAS USED HER GIFTS TO EDUCATE AND SPREAD POSITIVITY. SEASON 3 OF MADISON'S WIDELY SUCCESSFUL PODCAST, THE MADISON JAYE SHOW, NOT ONLY INTRODUCED HER FANBASE TO NEW CONCEPTS BUT GIVES A VERY REALISTIC GLIMPSE OF HOW THE MIND, BODY AND SPIRIT WORK, THROUGH THE LENS OF NILA 3019.......

INTERVIEW BY NOVIA ROSE

MADISON
JAYE

CREATING SPIRITUAL & GENERATIONAL WEALTH

— **WITH MADISON JAYE**

interview by NOVIA ROSE
Photo by NOTORIOUS PHOTOS

"This"This is coming full circle for me. Back in December when we recorded, we kind of predicted a lot of the things that are happening now. You introduced the world to my first personality with Spotify. and now we are on iHeart and in partnership with Pandora. After we released the first 3 episodes. Nila went back to 3019 for a bit. Now she's back.

"Basically this is about the future of Technology. Spirituality & Fashion. When we think of the future, we have to think of the trinity, the three that connect everything. These are the 3 pioneers of what's to come. so you just have to be conscious of everything, as far as what you're wearing, what you're doing, what you're saying and we're just going to bring it home with Spirituality for the rest of the season."

On The Reception Of Her Podcast and Thesis

"I think the Twin Flame thesis, was the one that I was kind of afraid to do because it was so vulnerable for me. Back in 2016/17 when I first started doing the spiritual research. and put out the concept of Twin Flames. there was really nothing about it at all on the internet. So I used to sit in the library, go off of vibrations of what I felt and I would literally have to look in books. After, we put out the first podcast. I was hospitalized for an anxiety attack (after Season 2). I never wanted to touch the topic again. God made me touch it the topic again. Unfinished business."

As she delved into more detail about her revisit to The Twin Flame topic. Madison outlined her updated thesis on it's connection to Christian Ideology. The New Twin Flame- A spiritual thesis challenging the concept of 'False Flames.' - A clear concise description of how the destiny of every Human being is already written. Madison adds instructions on how to achieve the greatest love....

"I don't believe in anything negative. I believe if you stay pure enough in a lifetime, then God can use you similar to how he used Jesus as a modern day profit to show what the purification in a lifetime can do. So a 'False Flame'. I like to call that the BC flame because I don't believe anything is false because it has a negative notation to it...the BC flame is the one that destroys you. breaks you down. When you think about it, you have to die to be reborn again. so that's when you meet you AD flame, after death. The Goal is NOT necessarily be with a Twin Flame. The goal is to be with your 5D life partner whether its a soulmate or a Twin Flame."

Journalism

"When I putting out my thesis. as a journalist. I am also showing people that there are different forms of Journalism. Anyone that knows me knows that I'm very shy unless I'm around my people. I'd rather sit at home and study organs and healing. go to the library to look up spiritual thesis. that's what I like to do. When Madison and Nila come out. it's a different side of me."

that i'm introducing to the world. Like. Nila is all about Tech. she's a Digital Strategist. and she's from the future. Looking back. no one was doing futuristic trends and now it's everywhere... If you go into the thesis. I discuss a little bit of how our souls are being divided. This lifetime is very special. It is the FIRST lifetime where we no longer have two realities. Any lifetime before this. we were just balancing the 5D(Spirit realm; why we go to sleep) and 3D (Reality). That's the only two worlds we've had. Which is why I introduced the concept of NILA. We are now entering into 3 worlds. because look. that thing on your lap is collecting my voice and visuals. Technology is a world and we will never not have it again.

On Stepping Into Spiritual Journalism

"I say this as humbly as possible. there's really no lane for spiritual journalism. When we started back in 2013. I was doing PR and I was doing Digital Marketing. but there was no title for it YET. We didn't have that label. now we look back and we thought it was just PR. it was really pioneering digital marketing back then. That's also what I am doing now with spiritual journalism. I say this. again. as humbly as possible. I'm a vessel. I just want to keep living it. When I broke down the thesis into three parts (Written. Audio and Visuals). I told my people to make sure they listen and pay attention to my STRATEGY. There are different formulas to Spiritual Journalism so when God is using you. you have to let him. It's about tapping into YOU

A

BLACK DRESS FOR
ANY OCCASION

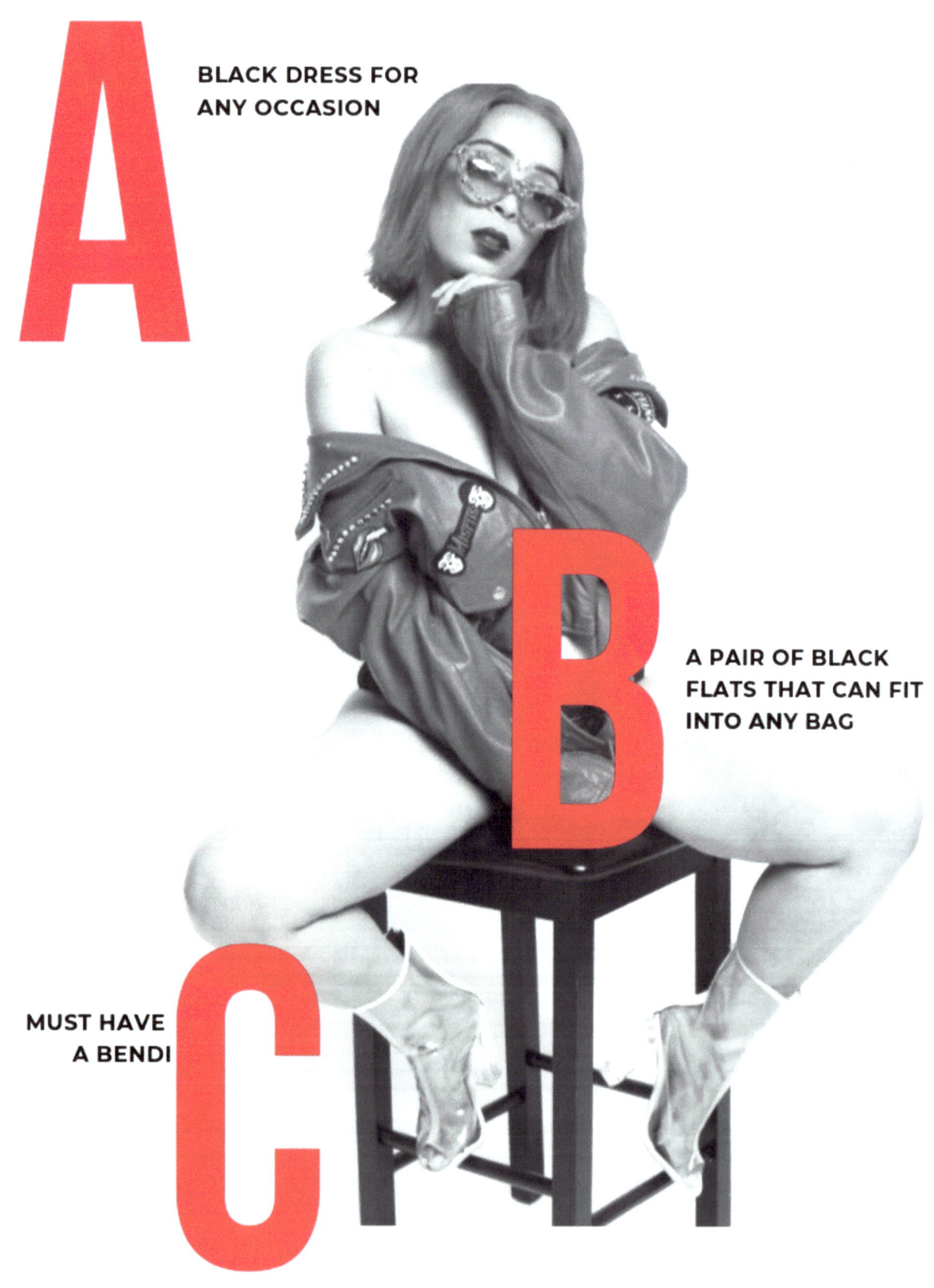

B

A PAIR OF BLACK
FLATS THAT CAN FIT
INTO ANY BAG

MUST HAVE
A BENDI

C

"WE ALL SHINE DIFFERENTLY, BUT WE ALL SHINE."

THE PODCAST PURPOSE

"BE YOUR FUCKING SELF BRO!" YOU ARE SO AWESOME. YOU ARE SO UNIQUE. AND I DON'T MEAN THAT IN A CHEESY WAY BUT WE ARE ALL SNOWFLAKES. THERE AREN'T TWO SNOWFLAKES THAT ARE THE SAME. IF YOU ARE TRYING TO BE SOMEONE ELSE, YOU CAN'T LIVE WHO GOD MADE YOU TO BE. WE HAVE ALL DECIDED TO COME INTO THIS LIFETIME TO SOMETHING SO FUCKING AMAZING, REGARDLESS TO WHAT IT IS. NO MATTER WHAT WALK OF LIFE YOU COME FROM, YOU ARE WORTHY. I COME FROM NOTHING. I ATE IN SOUP KITCHEN. I'VE SLEPT IN CARS WITH MY MOM AS A KID. I USED TO WALK MILES TO SCHOOL. I KNOW WHAT IT'S LIKE TO GO TO BED HUNGRY. I KNOW ALL OF THAT AND GOD HAS BLESSED ME. THAT'S HOW YOU KNOW IT'S SOMETHING HIGHER THAN ME — I DON'T CARE WHAT YOU'RE GOING THROUGH. GOD HAS SOMETHING SO AMAZING FOR YOU. ALL YOU HAVE TO DO IS TAP IN. EVERYBODY HAS A DIVINE PURPOSE. HEAL YOURSELF. WHEN I LEAVE THIS PLANET, I WANT TO LEAVE A LEGACY OF LOVE.

MADISON & NILA ARE GEARING UP TO HIT A CITY NEAR YOU IN 2020! IN THE MEANTIME, BE SURE TO KEEP WITH THE SPIRITUAL MEDIA MAVEN ON ALL SOCIAL PLATFORMS AND MADISONJAYE.COM!

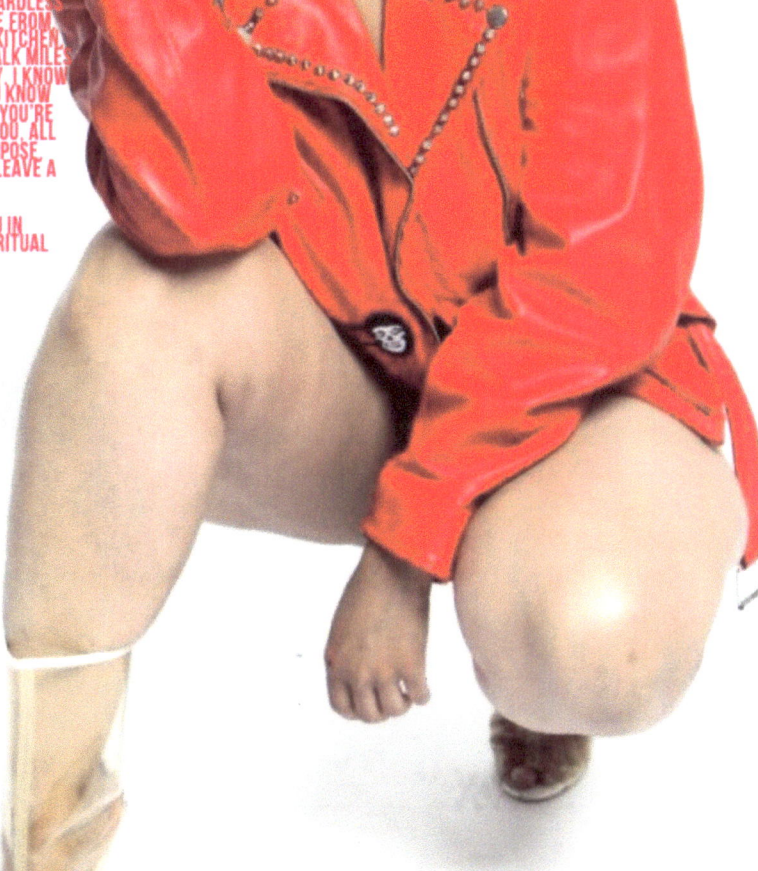

NOTORIOUS PHOTOS

THE HAIR SHIELD

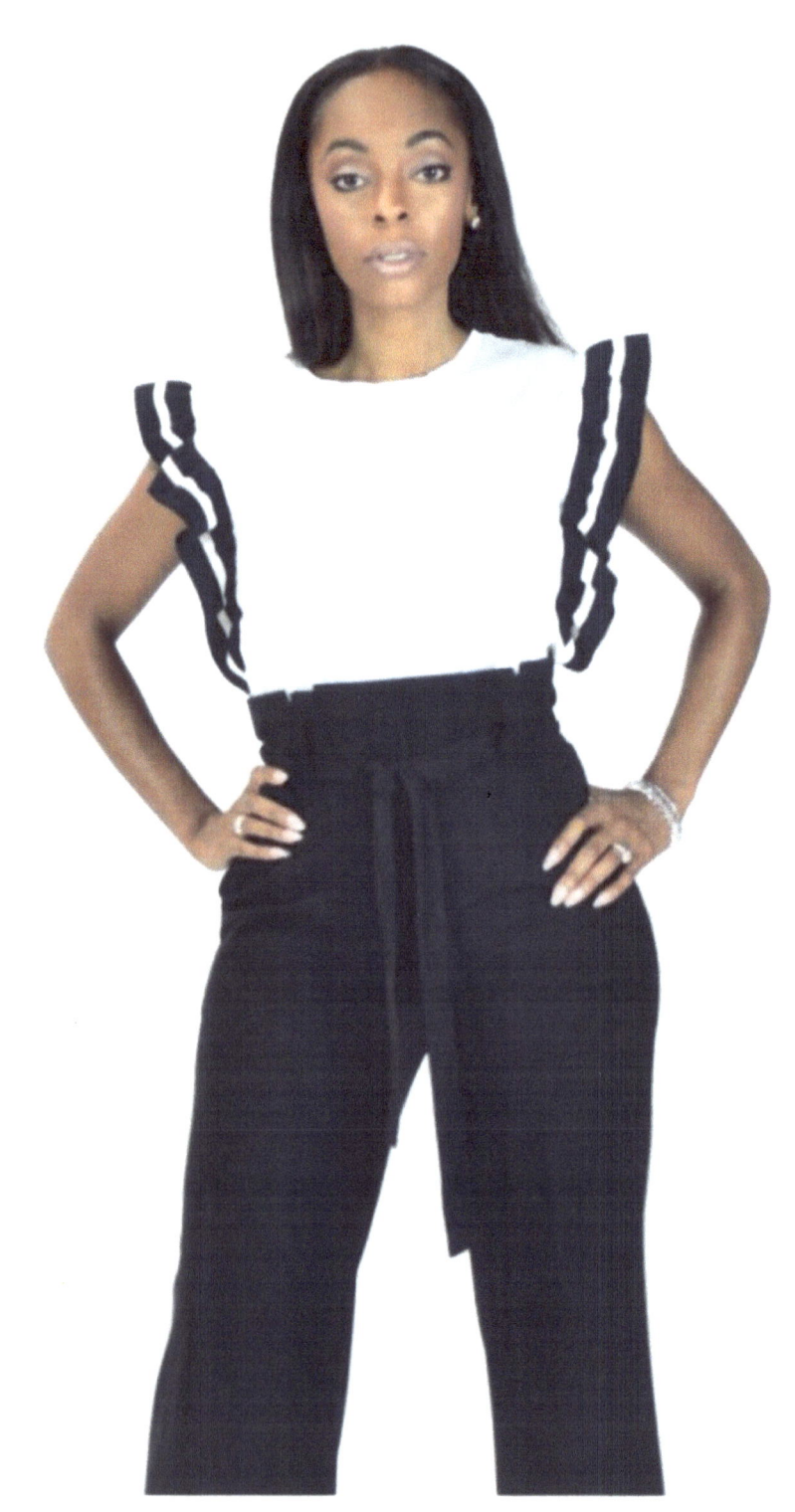

SATIN-LINED PROTECTIVE UNIT

The Hair Shield is a satin-lined protective unit that stores, transports and restores the beauty to your hair extensions. Its silky satin lining provides the optimal surface for storing extensions and ultimate quality preservation by reducing frizz and dryness. It is design with the frugal classy lady in mind.

Written by Freya Jimenez. IG: @thehairshield Fb: @thehairshield Twitter: @hair_shield

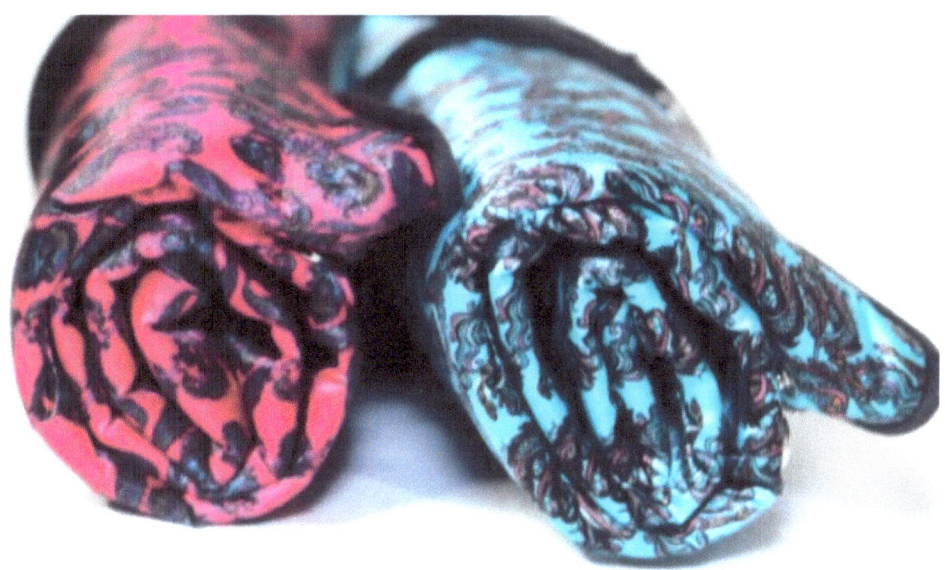

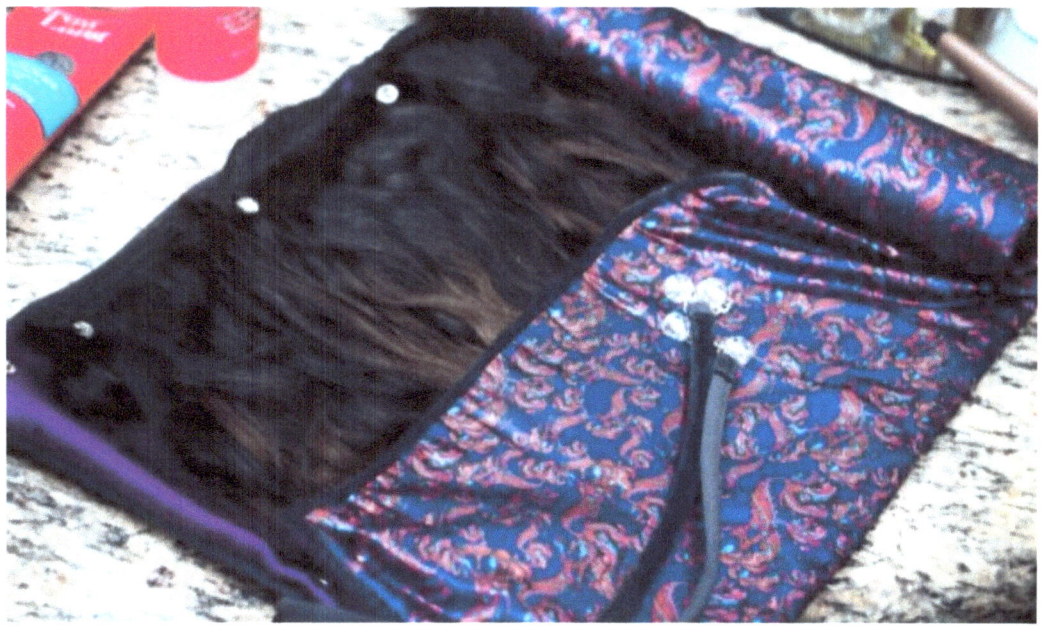

COVER
~~STORY~~

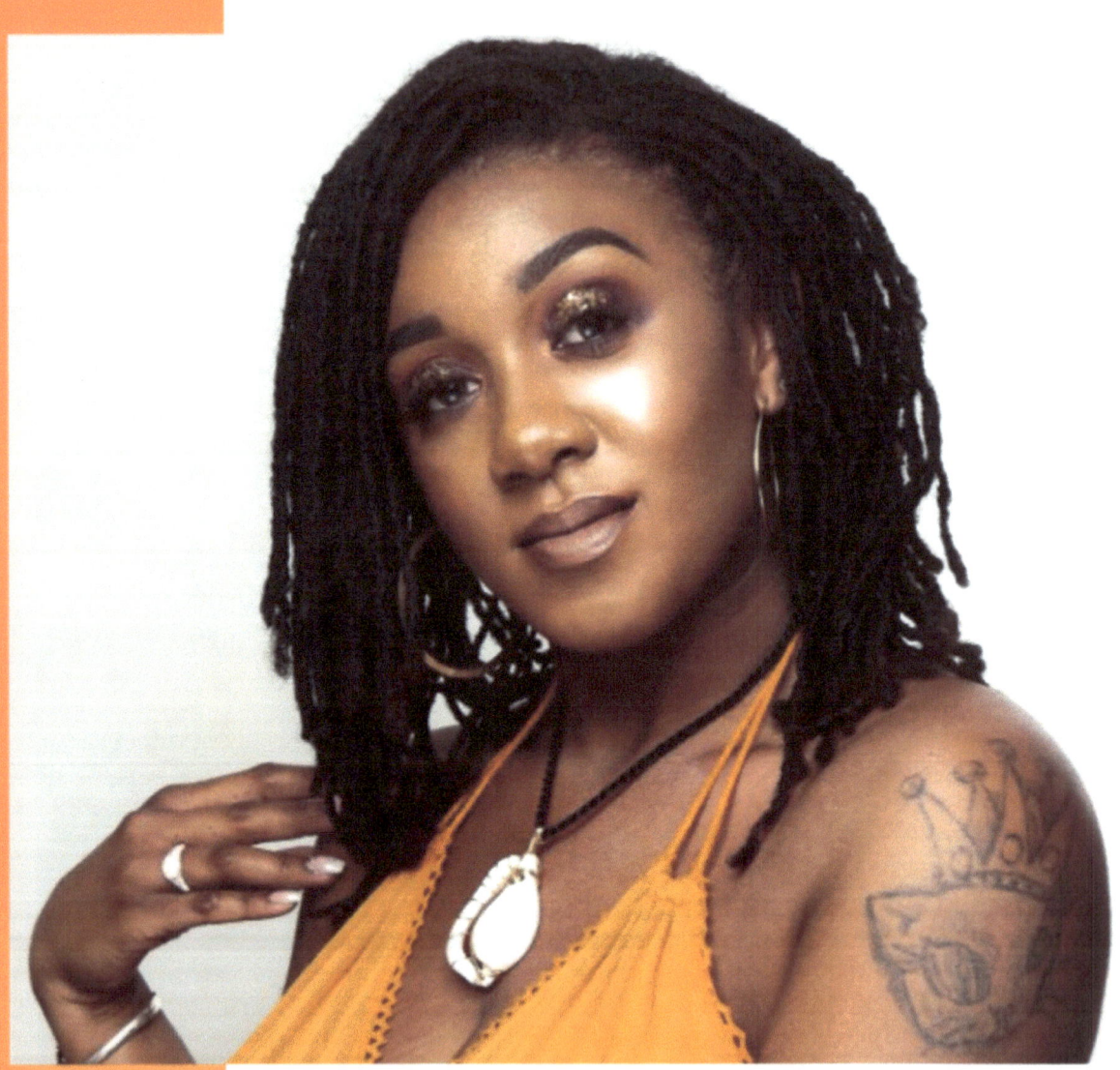

ALEXANDRIA
JEFFREY

CREDITS
MUA: SHANIEL TIRADO FROM SUPREME FACES
LLC (IG: SUPREMEFACES)
LASH ARTIST: JALORE LASHES (IG:
JALORE LASHES)
PHOTOGRAPHER: ADRIAN KING (IG:
WHOISADRIANKING
LOC JEWELS & NECKLACE: MAHOGANY
ROCHELLE (IG: @MROCHELLEJEWELS))

THIS ISSUE WE SAT DOWN WITH THE
AMAZING RISING BRAND EMPRESS LOCS &
BRAIDS. "WE AIN'T COME TO PLAY, WE CAME
TO SLAY!" IS THE COMPANIES MANTRA.
EMPRESS LOCS SPECIALIZES IN LOC, BRAIDS
AND CROTCHETS GOAL- HELPING OTHERS
FIND SELF CONFIDENCE THROUGH THE
MAINTENANCE OF THEIR CROWNS. WE SIT
DOWN WITH THE CEO BEHIND THE BRAND
FOR EXCLUSIVE ADVICE ON HOW TO MAKE A
BRAND IN THE HAIR BUSINESS . TAKE A LOOK
AT THE EXCLUSIVE TIPS BELOW.

COVER STORY

CREDITS
MUA: SHANIEL TIRADO FROM SUPREME FACES
LLC (IG: SUPREMEFACES)
LASH ARTIST: JALORE LASHES (IG:
JALORE LASHES)
PHOTOGRAPHER: ADRIAN KING (IG:
WHOISADRIANKING
LOC JEWELS & NECKLACE: MAHOGANY
ROCHELLE (IG: @MROCHELLEJEWELS1)

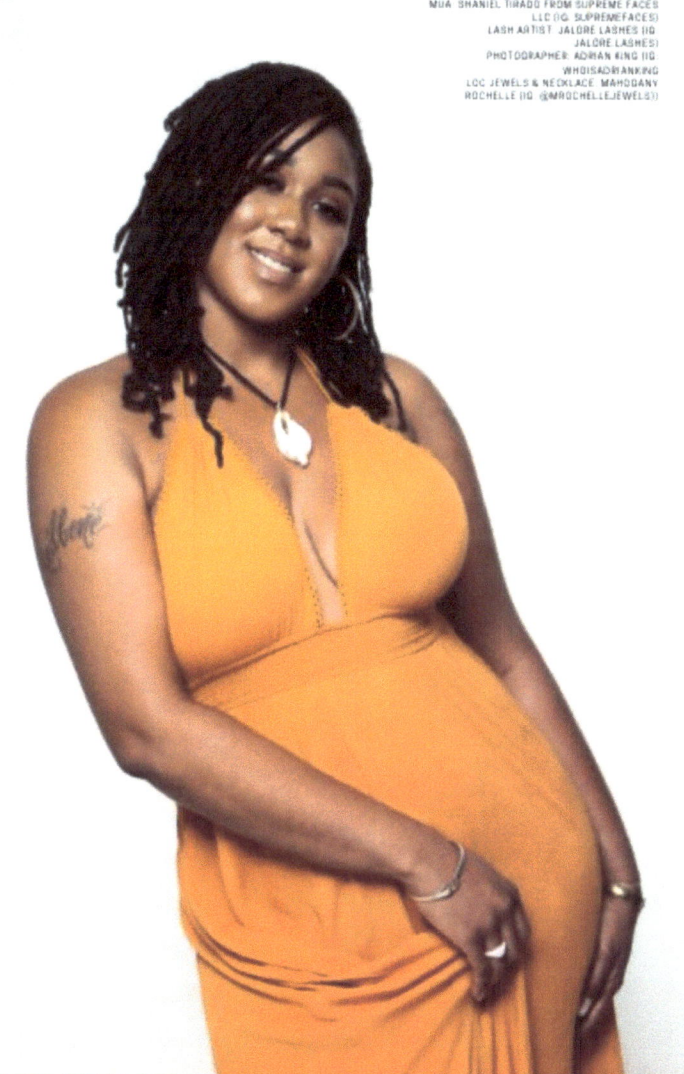

FGM: Its an honor to sit down with you all . Tell us a little about
your brand and how you've come to this vastly successful peek in
your career .
AJ: Thank you so much! Empress Locs & Braids is a Loc and Braid
Salon located in Orlando, FL at iStudio Salon Suites specializing in
Locs, Braids and Crochets. That will include Loc Maintenance via
Palm Rolling and the Interlocking method. Loc Repairs, Loc
Extensions, Brotherlocks, Feed In Braids, Box Braids and any
texture Crochet. I've come this far by working extremely hard
every single day, making sure my clients 100% satisfied after each
and every service. Network Marketing became a huge platform
and source of communication for me through social media as
well.

FGM: Who are the clients/what are the projects that you most
enjoy working on?
AJ: I love working with clients that keep on open mind about
learning self worth through their hair, as well as nurturing their
crown and the history of their hair. If I had to choose, it would be
working with Locs. It can be any type of maintenance, palm
rolling or interlocking. I'm here for it!

FGM: How do you feel you make a difference in the world?
AJ: I feel I make a difference in the world by helping others
impacting my client's lives by offering a listening ear or a helping
hand in any way I possibly can. Sometimes after speaking with
them, I feel like part of the family. This is how I build Loyalty, Trust
and Relationship with my clientele.

FGM: Tell us about a time when you showed determination to
continue as an entrepreneur
AJ: I showed determination as an entrepreneur at my lowest
moment when when I was ready to give up. I was terminated
from a call center job that I was working with for four and a half
years, had to relocate my home for safety reasons, so at the time I
was staying down South in Port St. Lucie with my mom but daily
traveling to Fort Lauderdale, Miami, West Palm Beach, Fort Pierce,
Daytona Beach, or Orlando for work because in Port St. Lucie.
there was no work for what I dreamed of. Every day I was traveling
from 5am to 2:00am or 3:00am in the morning. Sleep was the
least of my worries. One day I decided, whichever city shows me
the most love and support me, that's where I will lay my head.
Orlando was the city that won, ever since then I used PEOPLE as
my motivation to keep going.

FGM: Give me the three best qualities of your brand
AJ: Three best qualities are of my brand are Determination,
Loyalty and Hard Work

FGM: Give me an example of when you worked irregular hours?
AJ: I worked irregular hours during Memorial Day weekend. I
signed up to be part of the parade and festivities all weekend
long. I planned to have the weekend off to get myself ready but
instead I was out coloring hair at other's home. then later that
evening one of the girls from the troop for the parade flew in and
need her hair done. It was about midnight. I reopened the shop
and did her hair to go out to a party. I was down for the all
nighter. I believed I was done with her hair going on 3:00am in
the morning.

FGM: what are 5 tips you would give a rising entrepenuer ?
AJ: Tip One)Always stay true to yourself- Never ever forget where you
came from or how hard you worked to get where you are at this current
moment.
Tip two) Stay Positive- There are many days I feel like quitting, but I know
I can't. Too many people depend on me as to myself. Without positivity,
brings chaos. When you have chaos, you can't move forward.
Three)Patience- Being an entrepreneur doesn't happen overnight. There
are steps that needs to be executed before you can make it to the next
level or even the goal that you may have in mind. Patience is KEY.
Tip Four)Build your brand/name- This gives you constant credibility in
anything that you wish to accomplish.
Tip 5) Build a relationship with the ones that support you. This includes
keeping an open mind to new and challenging experiences.

FGM: Being a entrepreneur is a 24/7 job, how did you get ready for that?
AJ: There was no way I could have prepared for it. I will say working in the
fast food industry did help with standing on my feet for long hours as well
as multitasking. All my previous job has helped me with learning prestige
customer service and having people skills. For the most part, I take it one
day at a time, I never plan a full schedule, instead I let the day work itself
out because things are constantly changing around me.

FCM: How did you acquire the ability to work under pressure to beat meet deadlines as a entrepreneur ?

AJ: Meeting deadlines and working under pressure was definitely something that was a learning experience. I had to train myself to stay focused especially because my work hours ran so long everyday. I had to train myself to remain on task but at the same time don't get distracted and keep my clients fully engaged.

FCM: What is your favorite inspirational point, place, to develop new brand developments?

AJ: To develop new brand developments, my favorite inspirational point is viewing the cycle of life, viewing the everyday struggles that people go through and seeing if there's a way to make life a difference in their world or make them more confident while dealing with their lives.

FCM: Which current public figure, are you inspired by or appreciate the most?

AJ: I'm most inspired by Jesseca Dupart aka Judy (IG @darealbbjudy). She is such an inspiration! She owned a beautiful salon in New Orleans but it burned down. Today she is a millionaire owning her own brand of hair products, Kaleidoscope and a plaza in New Orleans. I love following her IG, viewing her ins and outs of building and up keeping her empire.

FCM: How do you handle stress ?

AJ: I handle stress by going through it. Stress makes me stronger and more efficient. I think a lot more clearly and deadlines are met.

FCM: FCM: What are the three qualities you feel an entrepreneur must have ?

AJ: I feel an entrepreneur must have patience, clarity, and confidence.

FCM: Where do you see your business in 10 years ? How do you plan to get there ?

AJ: In the next 10 years I see my business with 20 plus employees, a Hair Institute attached within a plaza that will help grow other small businesses grow and flourish. I plan on getting there by continuing building my brand and keeping an open mind to new business ventures.

FCM: It was a pleasure speaking with you thank you for joining us

AJ: Thank you so much for having me!

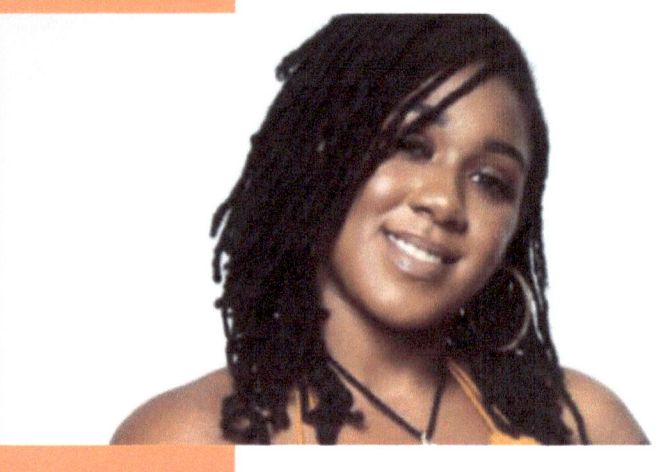

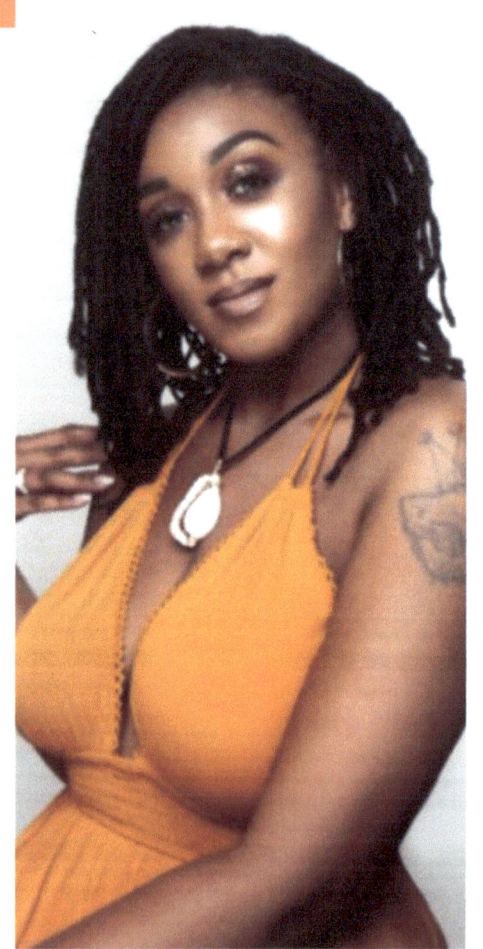

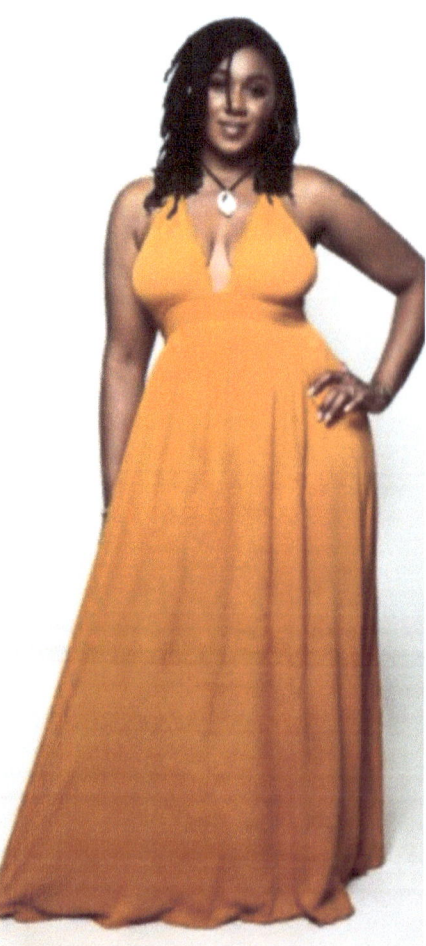

LIFE
WITH
THE EMPRESS

Inspiration & Fashion with ZLS Apparel

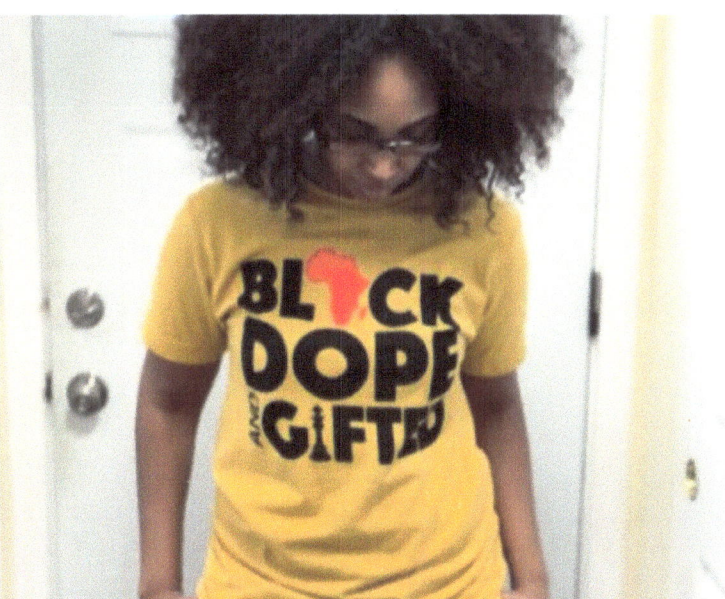

ZLS Apparel was inspired by 3 queens (our daughters) and came to fruition based solely on their livelihood. In fact ZLS is the first initial of their names, Zoey, Londyn, Sanai. We always wanted to set the example for our girls and show them that anything is possible through HARD WORK and FAITH! Through all of this we decided to come up with a BRAND that reflects us and our values and it be something that our girls and others can feel good about and apply to their everyday life.

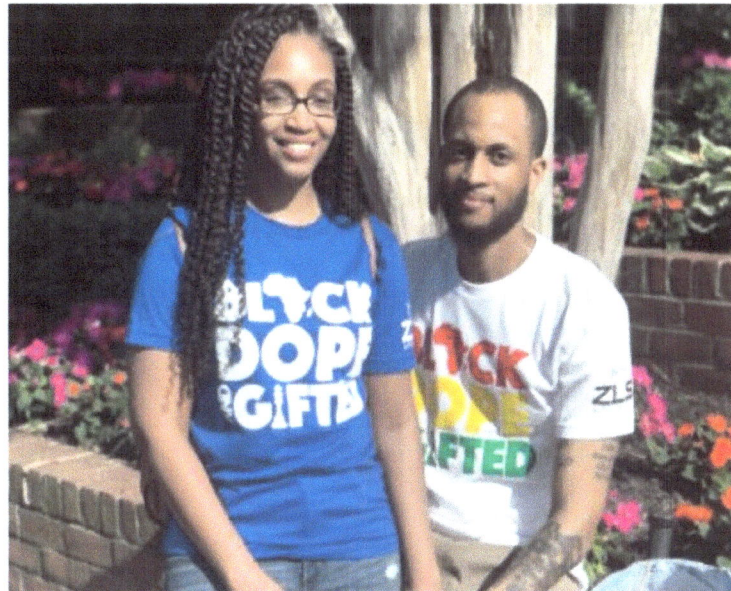

ZLS Apparel focuses on individuals having a sense of one's proper dignity, value; self respect by promoting PRIDE, POSITIVITY, and FAITH. ZLS Apparel is more than just a clothing BRAND, its a LIFESTYLE based on our core values to breed confidence and belief to the world while pushing fashion forward.

At ZLS Apparel we are a people focused brand that strives to promote a FAMILY vibe while working within our COMMUNITY to spread as much POSITIVITY as we possibly can!

-The ZLS Apparel Family!

@zlsapparel (Instagram)
@zlsapparel (Facebook)

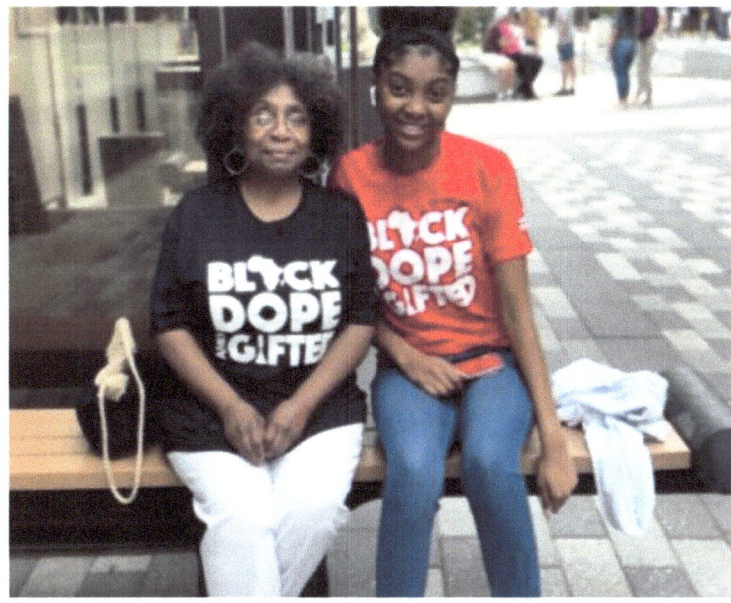

Mariah CEO of Shady Glam

BORN AND RAISED IN BALTIMORE, MARYLAND. MARIAH HAD A DREAM TO ALWAYS BRING CHANGE TO THE WORLD IN ANYWAY POSSIBLE. QUOTE FROM MARIAH CEO OF SHADY GLAM "BE CONFIDENT AND ALWAYS HOLD YOUR HEAD UP HIGH ON YOUR BEST OR WORST DAYS IN YOUR LIFE. YOU ARE SOMEONE SPECIAL DON'T YOU EVER FORGET THAT. FIX YOUR CROWN QUEENS AND KINGS AND KEEP PUSHING YOURSELF HARDER. NEVER STAY DOWN WHEN YOU FALL". FOLLOW MARIAH ON INSTAGRAM AT SHADY_GLAM (SHADY GLAM SHOP)

Tell us a little about your brand and how you've come to this vastly successful peek in your career .

•Answer: It is my pleasure to be apart of fashiongxdmagazine I appreciate the support from other black owned businesses/companies Including yours. My name is Mariah Milburn CEO of Shady Glam. Born and raised in Baltimore, Maryland. I am a 20 year old entrepreneur I sell shades,glasses and unisex necklaces. I am slowly adding newer products. Shady Glam was made November 2018. I got this bright idea to run my own business not knowing where to start. I am creative I have a list of business ideas on my phone and ipod I was made to be a billionaire/millionaire lol. I wanted to make cosmetic products and seen on Instagram this opportunity. This company helped other young entrepreneurs start for a reasonable price made logo,gave products ,created website for you as well. So why not take the opportunity? That is what I did. I didn't start off with cosmetics the package was for shades I took what I could get and could afford with her help and ended up getting a job again and expanding my business yearly.

FGM: Who are the clients/what are the projects that you most enjoy working on?
Answer: I love being able to create new ideas and put them into action.

FGM: How do you feel you make a difference in the world?
Answer: I inspire a lot of people. I inspire people who play like they don't see me. I inspire people who thanked me and I inspired my own family. I started my business to make a difference not by just selling products but also making it clear that I am always here for those who need advice,need to be uplifted and so on. Theres a good amount of people I came across with while being an entrepreneur.

Some of those people been through somethings I love to give up positivity, support,love and advice to anyone just so they'll understand they are IMPORTANT they have a purpose, it is not their final destination just a chapter and to never give up just because things don't go how we plan them. I love that I can help bring some type of change and spread the good things to the world.
FGM: Tell us about a time when you showed determination to continue as an entrepreneur.

Answer: Wow I have a few things to share. My business started when I was 18ish was close to my 19th birthday I started in November of 2018 my birthday is in December. When I started months went by I didn't make any sales I barely knew what I was doing but all I knew was I want to do this. I was getting discouraged often i thought about giving up until I got my first sale. It was only one of course but it was ok it was enough to help me feel good about my business. I made a few more sales this year 2019 wasn't a lot but was something. Everyday I think of how I started,what I started for and why. I been determined to not give up something I want to do and love doing just because of the money not coming in fast. I continued my entrepreneur journey and I feel good about it.

FGM: Give me the three best qualities of your brand
Answer: Confidence, Inspirational and Unique.
FGM: Give me an example of when you worked irregular hours?
Answer: I don't have an example.
FGM: Being a entrepreneur is a 24/7 job, how did you get ready for that?
Answer: Well I am also a college student I want to be a Pediatrician. On the side I run a business and was juggling a job as well. I didn't really get ready I believe whatever I am determined to do anything in my way will get crushed due to me having so much passion for things so I guess it was already in me I never prepared for it things just fell into place.

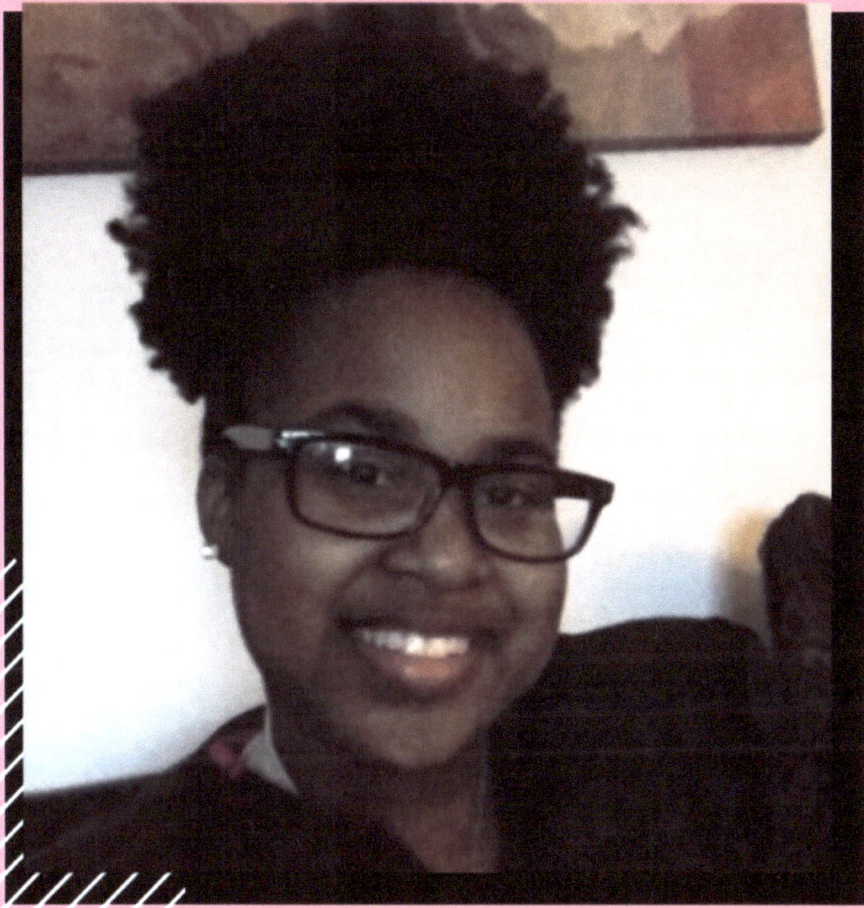

FGM: How did you acquire the ability to work under pressure to beat meet deadlines as a entrepreneur ?

Answer: Ummm. I honestly think being positive, surrounding myself with good vibes and knowing exactly what I am attempting to accomplish helps me hold myself together to get things done. I have moments where I get discouraged but I tend to snap myself out of it.

FGM: What is your favorite inspirational point, place, to develop new brand developments?

Answer: My room lol watching certain videos just gets my creative juices flowing or even randomly being out seeing certain things I'll get inspired to create something.

FGM: Which current public figure, are you inspired by or appreciate the most?

Answer: I don't really have one. I save things from these lovely people instagrams such as meek_university,Gary vee, ace metaphor, the hustler university ,the branding bar. And I appreciate exclusive.minks my entrepreneur friend she has helped me through somethings with my business and helped motivate me she inspires me a lot.

How do you handle stress ?

"Make sure it is something you love doing not a like. Everything you like can change in a split second."

MAKE SURE YOU ARE CONSISTENT AND COMFORTABLE WITH EVERYTHING FIRST AND FOREMOST. BE CONSISTENT, DRIVEN, ON YOUR A GAME DAILY.

BY AMELIA PERKINS

Answer: I watch positive affirmations,music,sleep,jot down new ideas for businesses and ASMR. Not to mention I have a very supportive boyfriend on my side a supportive friend and last but not least awesome small business entrepreneurs that I associate with often who inspire me and we motivate and keep one another in good spirits. Remember to always have good people in your corner.

Theres going to be strangers rooting for you giving you a push to be your better self. Never look for support from anyone. SUPPORT YOURSELF ALWAYS. The ones you look to for anything be the main ones never there for you when you need it. BE SUPPORTIVE OF YOURSELF and accept that it is ok for blood,friends and so on to not be rooting for you take that in and keep going allow that to be your fuel to keep going!!

FGM: What are the three qualities you feel an entrepreneur must have ?

Answer: Patience, Confidence and to be Determined and Driven.

FGM: Where do you see your business in 10 years ?How do you plan to get there ?

Answer: I see my business expanding into something more than just a online store. I want to open up a store front one day and hire good ,respectful can be trusted people. I'll actually plan to get there by improving on my craft more and more daily.

FGM: It was a pleasure speaking with you thank you for joining us

Answer: Thank you very much for allowing me to be a part of this. I support my black owned businesses/companies.

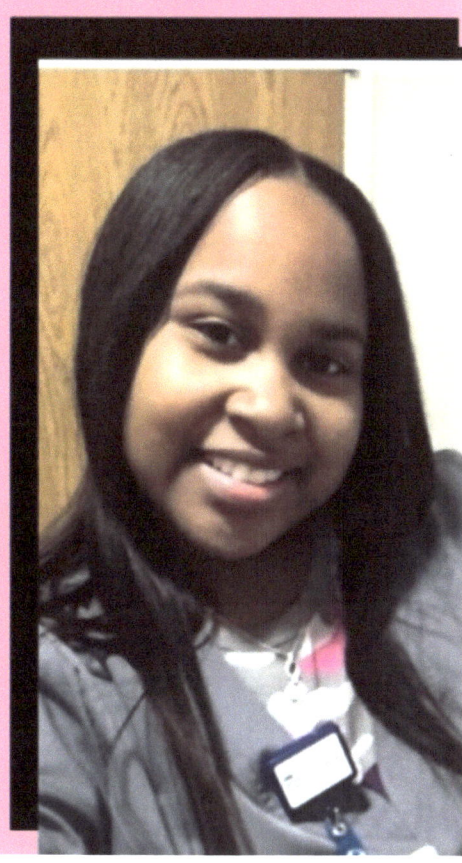

CANDICE'S

Snap Chat, Twitter, and Instagram
@lilmissent. Follow Awesome Nobody on
Twitter @awesomenobdy and Instagram
@awesome_nobody17
YouTube channel The Little Miss Ent. Show.

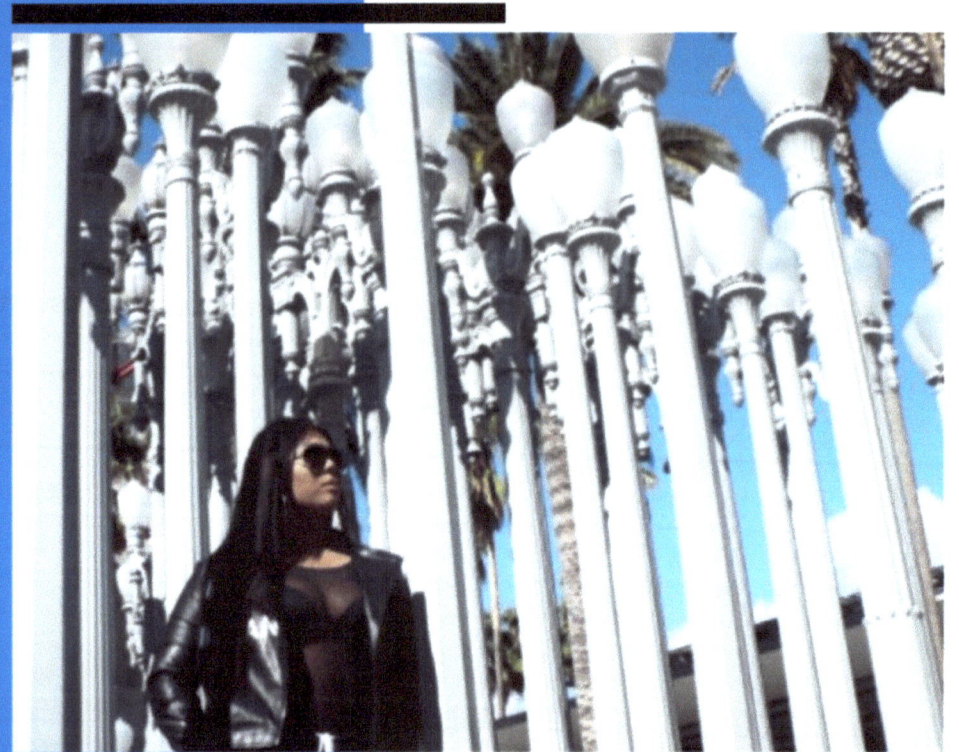

FIVE KEYS
TO BEING A
SUCCESSFUL
PODCASTER

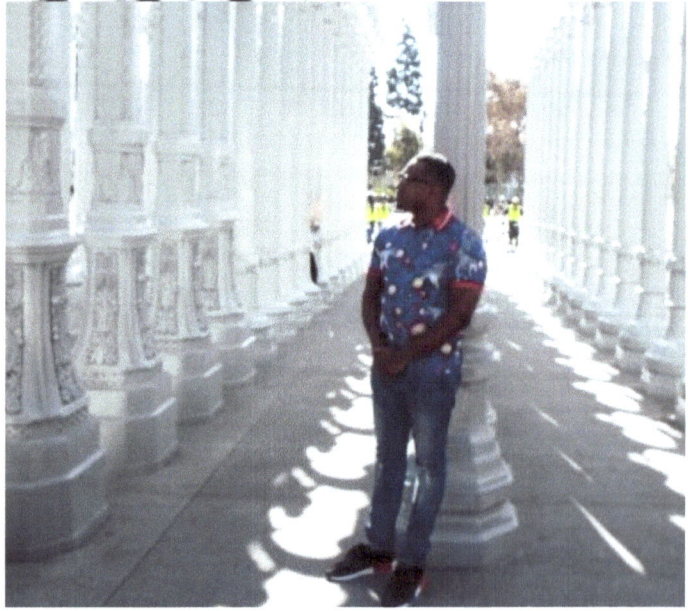

Candice is the host of The Little Miss Entertainment Show podcast. The podcast debut October 19th, 2015 and it is a must listen every Monday. Each show she interviews a guest. Her passion is allowing really amazing people to tell their really amazing story's. Also, her executive producer Awesome Nobody joins on their collaboration podcast "The Wedding Edition" documenting their recent engagement and planning their wedding together. Finally, catch the duo periodically on their spin off podcast "The Catch Up". During these episodes they share thoughts on Pop Culture, Music, and whatever the heck else is going on in the world.

Candice goes by the name Little Miss Entertainment because that is exactly what she is. She is a 10+ year executive in the entertainment business. She has worked with everyone from Kevin Hart to the late great Ms. Aretha Franklin.
In a recent interview Candice explains "It gives me such joy to be able to do things to put a smile on peoples faces. I love everything from throwing surprise birthday parties for my family members to putting on music festival for thousands of people. I love to create unforgettable moments for people" Between spending time with her family and traveling the world Candice wants to share all of her experiences through her podcast. Here are Candice's five tip t being a successful podcaster.

1.) BE YOURSELF. IT DOESN'T MATTER IF THERE ARE 1,000 INTERVIEW STYLE PODCAST, I KNOW THAT HOW I CONDUCT MY INTERVIEWS IS SPECIAL TO MY LISTENERS. THAT'S ALL THAT IS IMPORTANT. IF YOU TOUCH ONE OR ONE MILLION YOU'VE DONE YOUR JOB!

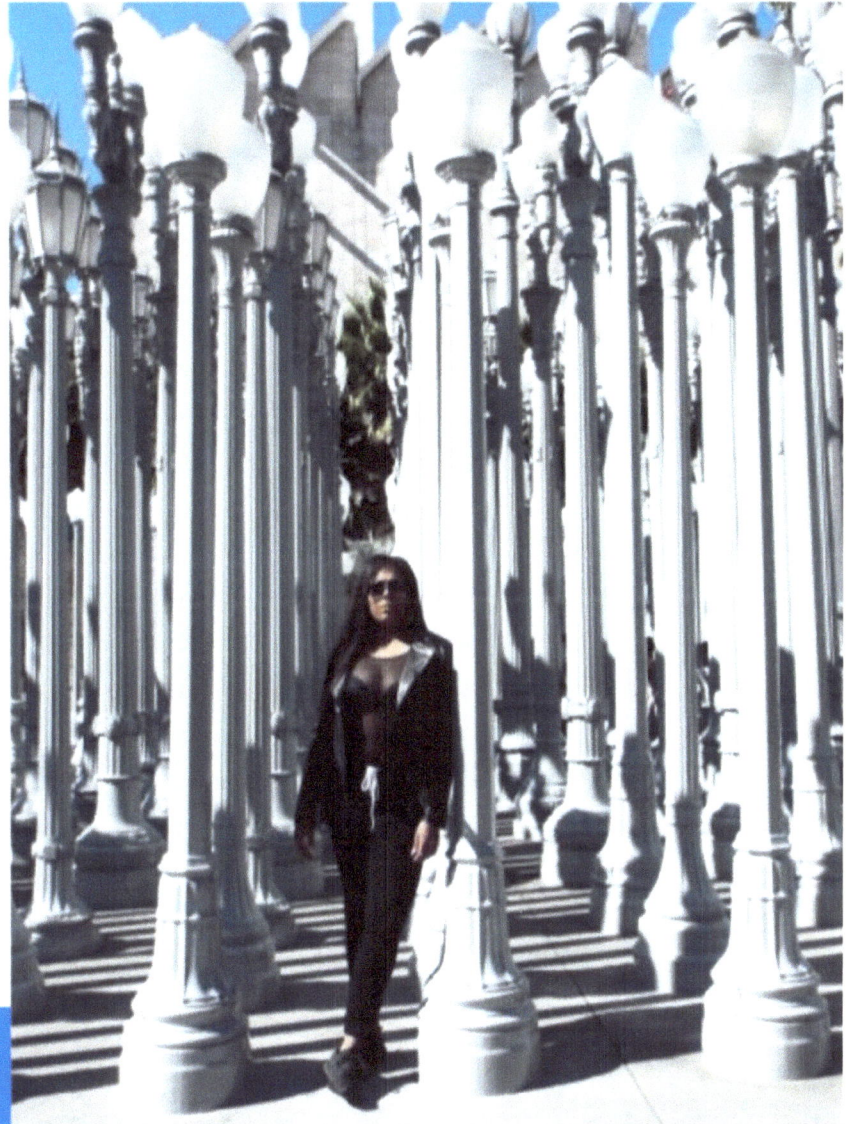

2.) Quality over quantity. Make great content that will last forever. A person should be able to binge your podcast from episode one and not think wow this is super dated. That doesn't mean don't talk about current events but, you should tie it back to something the listeners can learn from. Also, invest in good audio equipment. You don't have to break the bank to do so. Facebook market place is a gold mine for podcast equipment for cheap. Your listeners deserve to hear your content it is best form. Don't let them bed distracted by bad audio.

3.) Don't worry about the numbers. We live in a day in age where you can buy listens, followers, and likes. Don't worry about why you're not getting as many likes as the next podcast. worry about growing your brand awareness for other streams of revenue related to your podcast.

4.) Have merch! Podcast fans love to support and it's a great revenue stream. Also, wear your merch! You should be a walking billboard for your podcast. Be proud of what you created and broadcast it to the world. You never know who is watching. Also, support other podcast and they will support you too! It's nice to network with people with the same passion. If you see your fellow podcaster is selling merch to get money to book a venue to have a live podcast. support it! You will need that same support in return one day, trust me!

5.) Have an Executive Producer. It sounds fancier than it is but, it so important. Have a person that helps produce the show from a fresh set of eyes and different perspective. If you are the host you are a creative which in turns means you're a creative. And....creatives are sensitive about their work. You need someone to pick it apart and put it back together in its greatest form. I am blessed that my best friend, fiancé, and co-host Awesome Nobody is my Executive Producer. He is the engine that keeps the Little Miss Entertainment Show running. He schedules the interviews, edits the audio, researches the latest technology, maintains the YouTube channels, scouts the venues for the live shows, and DJs all our events. He is beyond amazing but, most importantly he sees the vision and he keeps me grounded. We are a team and every successful podcast needs a team!

Honorable Mention: Shout our your followers. My best friend Brittney told me once "Love Those Who Love You!" It was no truer words spoken. Your friends aren't your fans. They are people that love you for things outside of the podcast. They are bias. It's the person in your DM's from 5 states away your never met. They will tell you helped them through one of the toughest times in their life because they listen to your podcast today. That person deserves to be celebrated because that support is so real! I close everyone show by saying, I love you for listening because 100% you didn't have to." I mean that from my heart. My supporter are the reason I continue to challenge myself to be the best podcaster I can be.

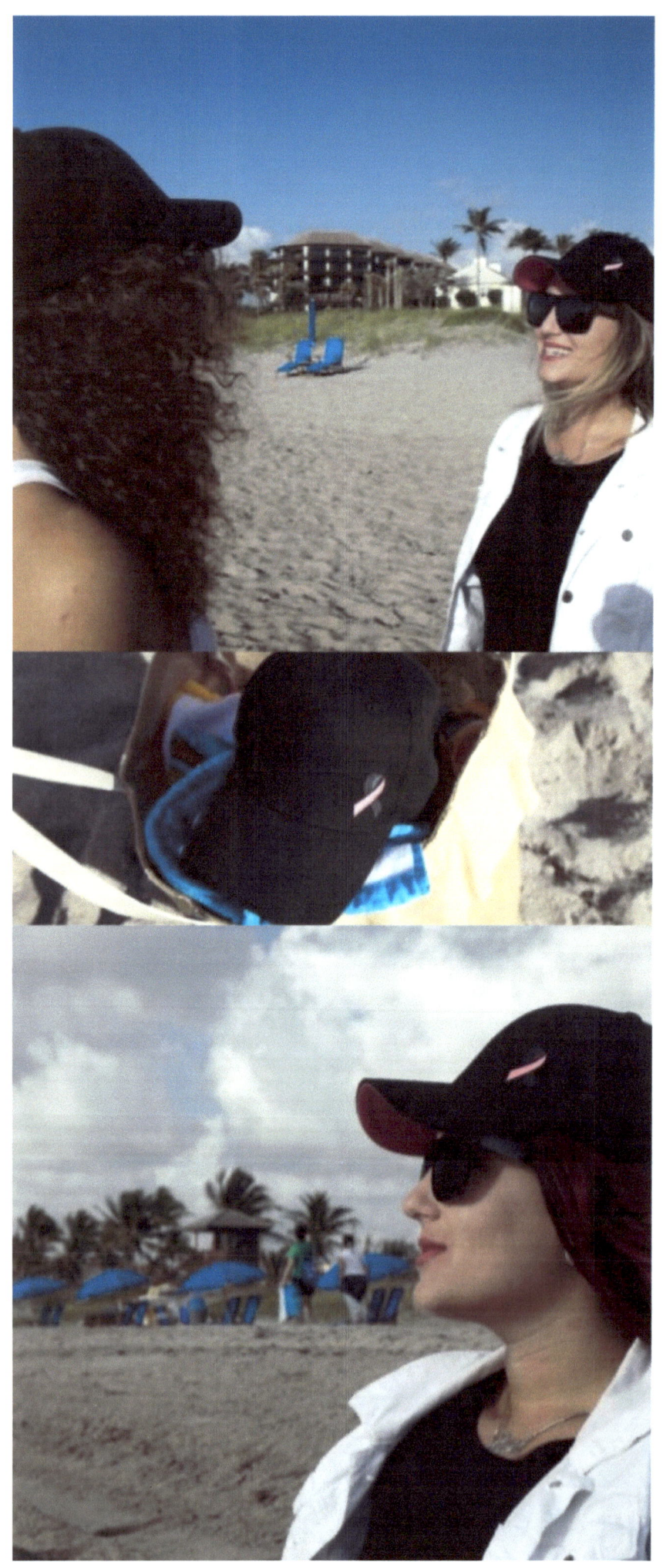

Hats On Hats Off,

By Karl Plenton
Instagram: @hatson.hatsoff
Facebook: @hatson.hatsoff
Website: www.hatsonhatsoff.com

My name is Paige Beattie and I am the founder of Hats On, LLC and Hats Off, Inc.

Hats On is a for-profit company that sells cancer awareness hats. Twenty (20%) percent of the proceeds are donated to the sister non-profit, Hats Off. Hats Off raises money through Hats On and outside donations to purchase wigs and other headwear for cancer patients in need. Each cancer patient receives two wigs - a day-to-day wig and a fun and funky wig or headwear. Our hope is to put some enjoyment into what is a gloomy and scary time.

By promoting Hats On, I want to raise awareness for all the cancers that affect people every day. So many people are unaware of the many types of cancers that people suffer from and I want to escalate that awareness level. As for Hats Off, I want to bring some pleasure into the chemo experience. Yes, this is a time when cancer patients are losing their hair, but now is the time to wear the crazy, fun wigs and express themselves differently in a way they may have always wanted.

My inspiration to start these companies lies with my mother, as she was first diagnosed with breast cancer 15 years ago. Once she started going through chemo and losing her hair, she went wig shopping. Although I was young, I remember her coming home in tears because of the experience she had. It was already a tough time and the people who helped her get a wig made her feel even worse about herself, not to mention the price tag. I am also proud to say that when she recently was diagnosed again and started chemo, she was Hats Off first donee.irst donee.

"BRINGING BACK, BUYING BLACK"

Written by Lavendar Hansen

SOCIAL MEDIA:
TBD_FASHION
BLACKDOLLARFASHION.COM
#BLACKDOLLARFASHION

The Black Dollar Luxury Clothing is a brand based around one phrase: "BUY BLACK". Originated in 2018, TBD Luxury Clothing is branched off of "The Black Dollar", a Network (Co-ed "Sorority Fraternity" for Black Business Owners) that also created a FREE to use platform that allows everyone to interact with Black Owned Businesses throughout the U.S!

Their styles are extravagant, revolutionary, & fly, giving you the ability to look good AND stand up for what we believe in! 'We, Are, Fashion', speaks for all black people: 'We' shape the culture, 'We', decide what's fire and what's not, but 'We' don't profit from it as much as we should" says the Creative Director, "We're here to change that"

The concepts, designs, & clothing are created by South Bronx, NYC native, Aaron Summers. "NYC set the tone in everything, from music, to fashion, & art. My family also played a big part in my sense of style: I watched my mother make us & other people clothes (one of her 10 hustles to help pay bills), and thought the process & creativity was dope. My father was just a naturally clean fly guy with the Biggie mobster type suits, and my big sis, who also designs & owns her own fashion line "Corqseru" (@_corqseru_), was pretty much my stylist growing up. My younger brother (Photographer, @exq_image) never gave a f*** about what anyone thought. I always respected & used that in life & my thought/creative process for everything. Check out their latest "LBTC" (Live By The Code) pieces from their "Summer Vibes" Collection & order now on blackdollarfashion.com!

Cut out the noise - Don't listen to anyone who offers negativity without a solution
All in or nothing - "You can't get to 2nd base if your foot's still on 1st"
Move how you would if your brand was worth millions TODAY
BE GRATEFUL - Take time EVERYDAY to focus and give thanks for what you have right now (best times are when negative complaining thoughts come to your mind)
"Patience -Perseverance - Prosperity"

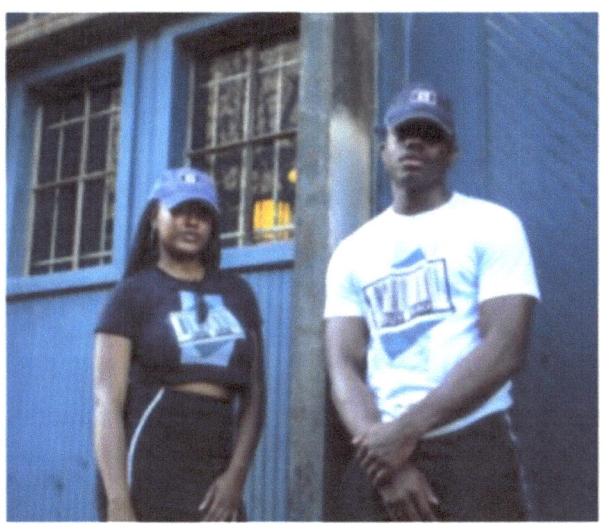

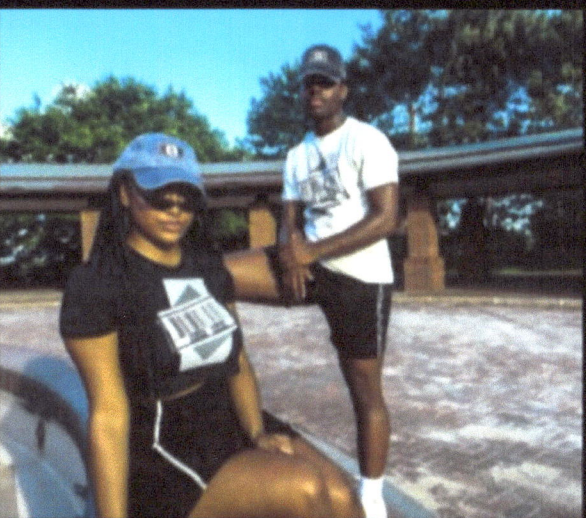

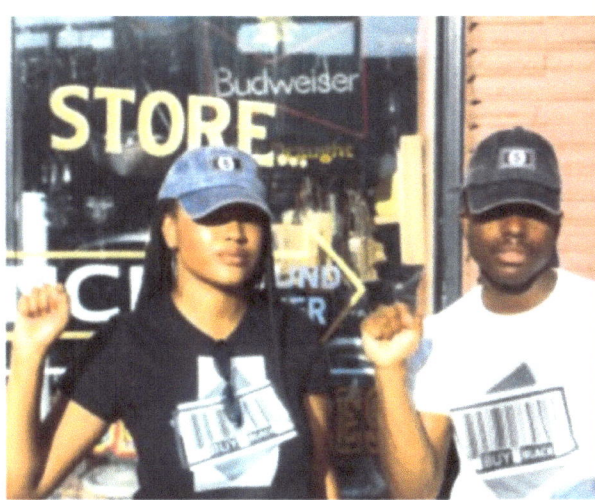

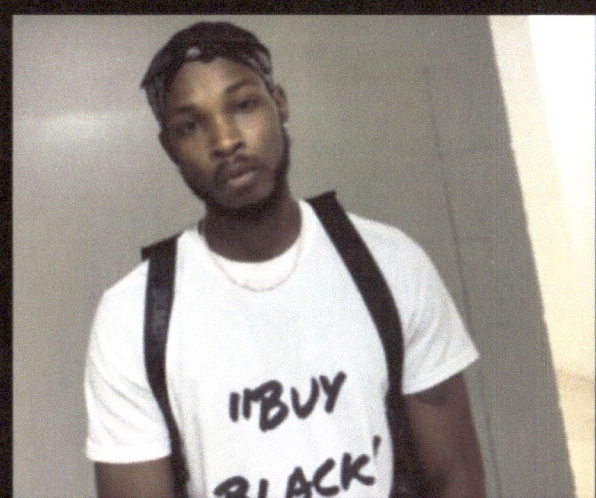

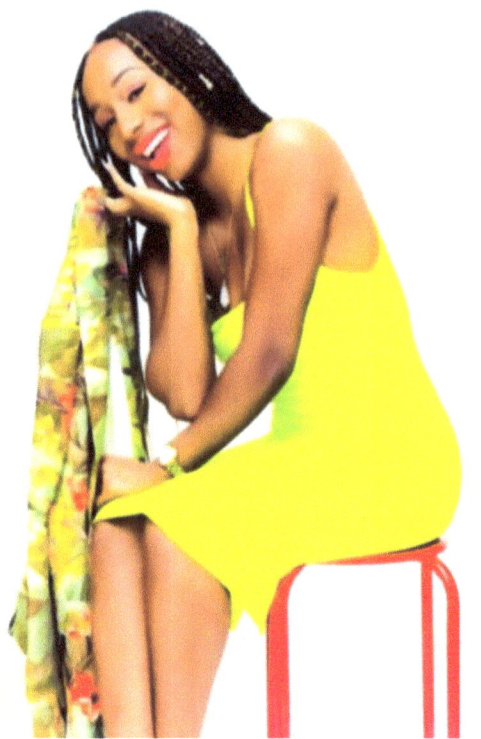

Inspiring different places

This week we sat down with an amazing rising brand Inspired by Ibrena. Inspired by Ibrena is an inspirational, self care brand. Being a personal brand where they currently offer inspirational messages in the forms of Greeting Cards, Life Coaching Personalized Quotes, and Self Care Blogs. Get the exclusive interview with Fashion Gxd Magazine on the brand phenom.

Social media accounts
www.inspiredbyibrena.com
Instagram: @transparenttrin
(Blog) // @inspiredbyibrenallc (Life Coaching)
@inspiredbyibrenacards (Greeting Cards)

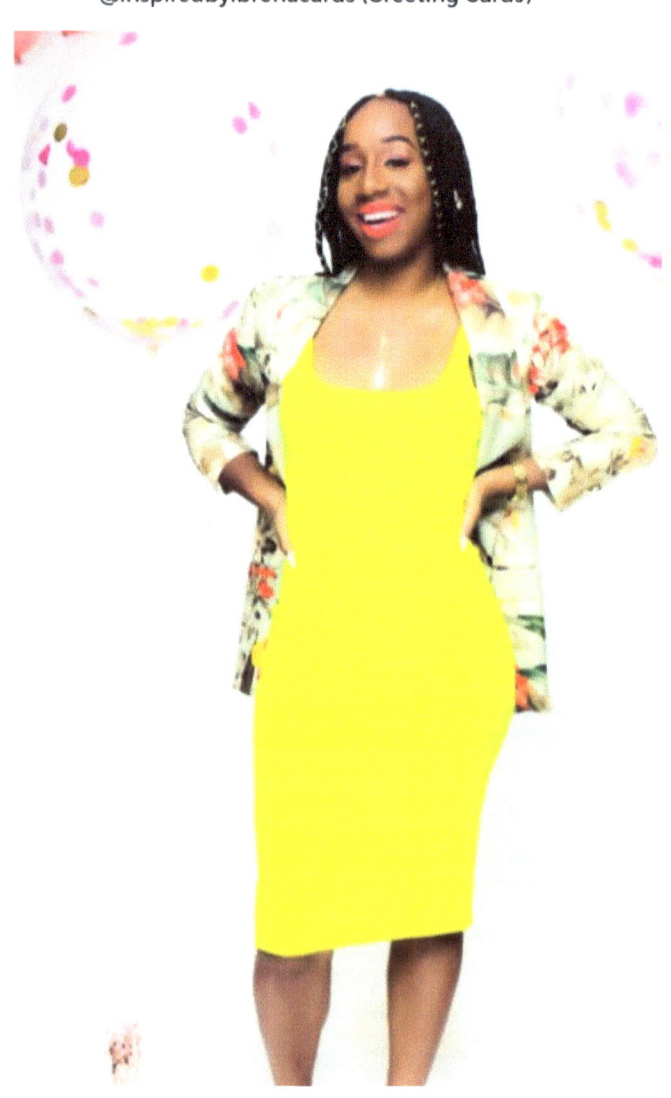

Fashion Gxd Magazine : How did the idea for your business come about?

Answer: Inspired by Ibrena Life Coaching began through my love for connecting with others and talking about their goals, life, obstacles, passions, and struggles. I believe these conversations allow for hue-mans to share and support one another along their journeys throughout life; they help people grow and evolve.

From conversations with millennials like myself and social media observations, I noticed that we all have this desire to be great, live our best lives, and reach our fullest potential. I've been able to create my own reality and success for myself, so I want to help millennials like me, do the same for themselves.

Inspired by Ibrena Greeting Cards came from my constant struggle to find greeting cards on holidays and birthdays that could depict common black situations, such as a Mother's Day Cards for your grandmother who raised you, or a card with an image of a black person on the front. I was inspired by this issue and decided to be the change I wanted to see. Thus, Inspired By Ibrena Greeting Cards were birthed.

Fashion Gxd Magazine : How do you find people to bring into your organization that truly care about the organization the way you do?

Answer:

As of now, Inspired by Ibrena is a one woman show, with the exception of my graphic designer who executed my vision for my greeting cards. My business is fairly new and I intend to employ family and friends who already genuinely support my business.

Fashion Gxd Magazine : What three pieces of advice would you give to other children who want to become entrepreneurs?

1. Don't just "ride the wave" of entrepreneurship because it seems "cool." Know why you're choosing this route and create a business that is a true reflection of "you," not just selling the next cool product or service.

2. Go into your business with pure intentions and focus on using your unique gifts to bring value to others.

3. Respect the process. Do not expect a "success" story overnight. You must put forth the time, energy, and effort in order to see growth.

Inspired by Ibrena

Fashion Gxd Magazine :If you had the chance to start your career over again, what would you do differently?

Answer: My actual career is an educator. I do not regret my career choice. It has perfectly prepared me for my business as a life coach and has provided many transferable skills, which assist me in running my business. Entrepreneurship was never my plan, but everything is aligning perfectly, as I transfer from full time educator to full time CEO.

Fashion Gxd Magazine :What would you say are the top three skills needed to be a successful entrepreneur ?

Answer: 1. Patience 2. Self -Discipline 3. Time Management

Fashion Gxd Magazine :What have been some of your failures, and what have you learned from them?

Answer: I honestly wouldn't consider anything I've been through a 'failure' more like a lesson. I'm new to entrepreneurship and the best way to learn is to try, make mistakes, and learn from them. The greatest lesson I've learned is to really plan ahead and allow myself time for marketing and mistake making. When I've cut my deadlines too close, a minor hiccup can cost me. I must plan ahead for the unknown.

Fashion Gxd Magazine : How many hours do you work a day on average?

Answer: This definitely varies based on whether it's holiday season for my greeting cards and how many clients I have for my life coaching at the moment. It's definitely a daily, full time job.

Fashion Gxd Magazine :Describe/outline your typical day?

Answer: My typical day consists of waking up, meditating, reading something positive, going to my full time career as an educator sending emails on my break whether it be to clients, my graphic designer, or social media marketing.
I go the gym afterwards, ship greeting cards, more social media marketing and engagements, brainstorming new cards,creating content, coaching clients, and I end my day by journaling and reading a good book.

Fashion Gxd Magazine : How has being an entrepreneur affected your family life?

Answer: I'm single with no children, so there hasn't been a profound affect on my family life; however, my siblings and other relatives are extremely proud and inspired by my decision to pursue entrepreneurship.

Fashion Gxd Magazine :What motivates you?

Answer: I'm motivated by my siblings and the positive responses I receive when I see a video of someone excited from receiving an Inspired By Ibrena Greeting Card with a picture of black person on the front who represents them. I'm also motivated by my clients positive responses when they tell me how my coaching has allowed them to realize things about themselves they didn't know and make meaningful changes in their lives.

Fashion Gxd Magazine: How do you generate new ideas?

Answer: All of my ideas are generated from my experiences in life and my intuition, whether it be the concept for Inspired By Ibrena Greeting Cards, a topic for my reflective blog "L's Into Lessons," or the guidance I provide my clients through Inspired By Ibrena Life Coaching.

Fashion Gxd Magazine : What sacrifices have you had to make to be a successful entrepreneur?

Answer: The greatest sacrifice I've made is how I utilize my time and finances. I had to teach myself that I'm not losing time or money, I'm making an investment into myself and brand, which is well worth it.

Fashion Gxd Magazine : Where you see yourself and your business in 10 years? 20 years?

Answer : In 10-20 years Inspired By Ibrena Greeting Cards will be the largest, black, woman owned greeting card company in the US. I will be the Iyanla of Life Coaching for Millennial Women, with a show on OWN. My blog "L's Into Lessons" will have inspired millions and allow me to travel around the world as an inspirational speaker.

Kreyòl Cosmetics

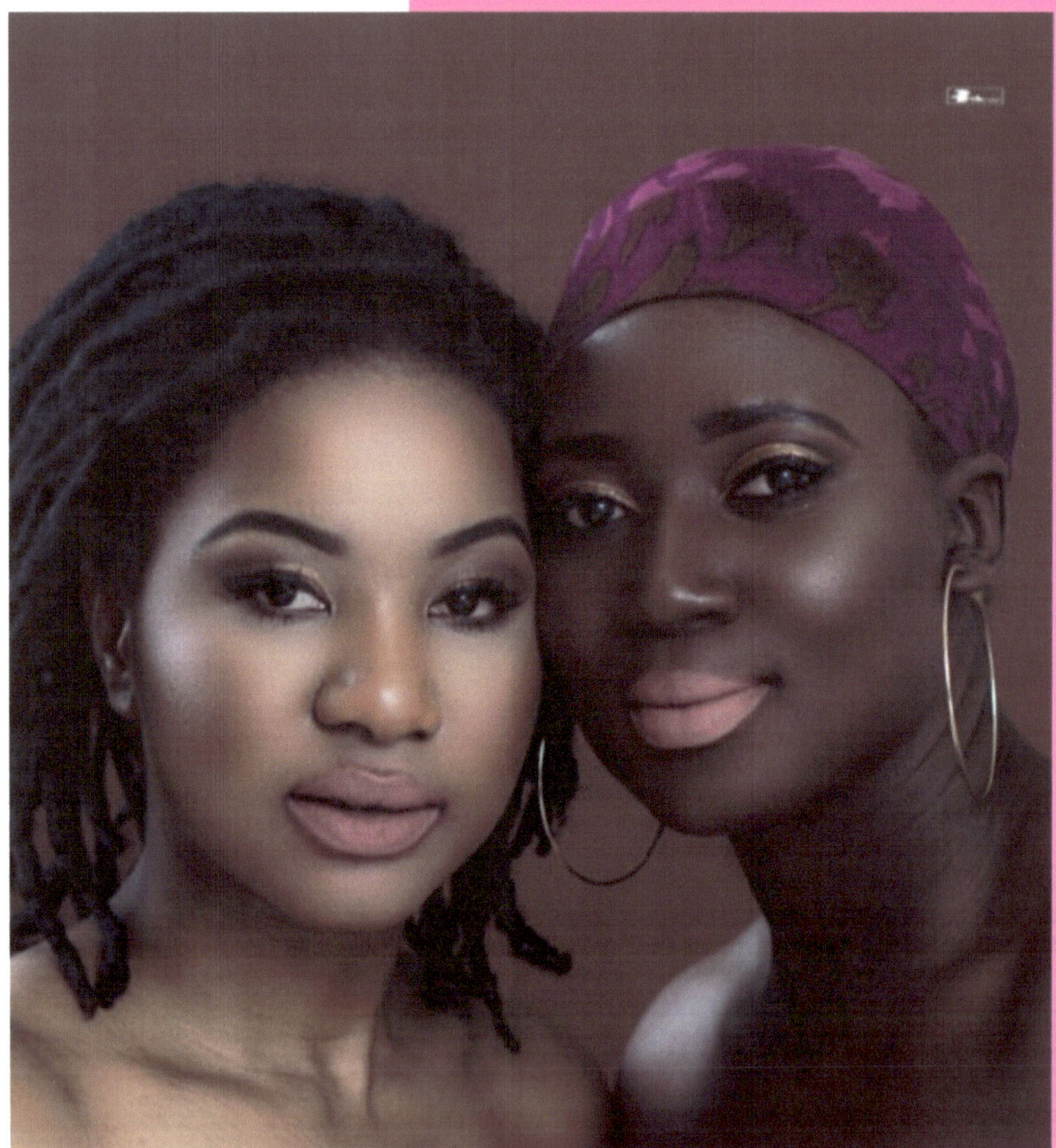

Instagram / Twitter @kreyolcosmetics / www.kreyolcosmetics.com

Kreyòl Cosmetics is a unisex vegan brand founded by a cosmetic chemist, we are about community, self-improvement and transparency. All of our products are formulated with love and care, we want everyone's experience with us to be a positive one.

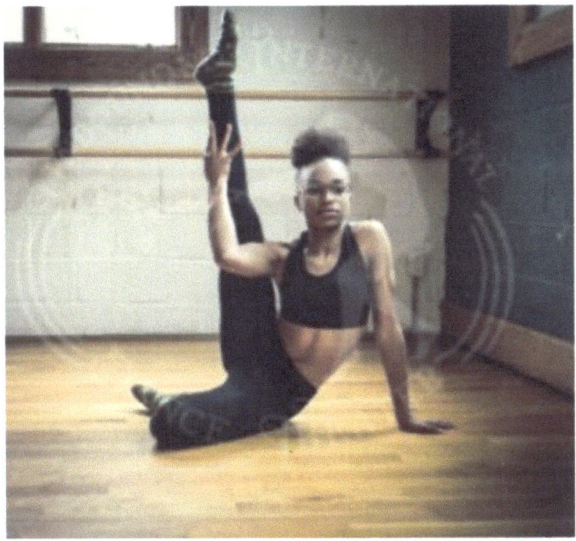

DANCER: JERRICKA MCCLUE.

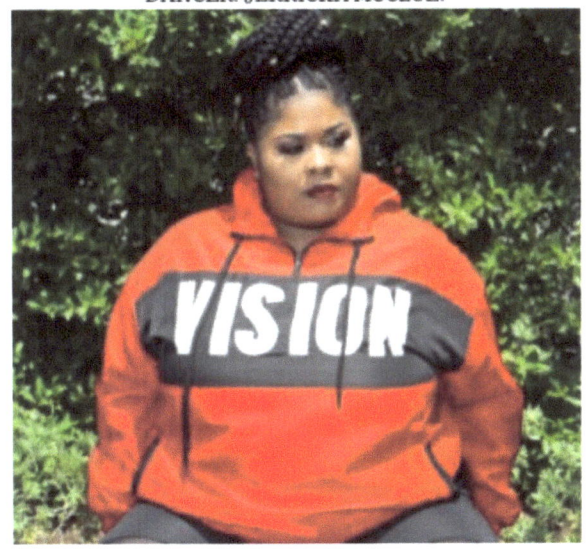

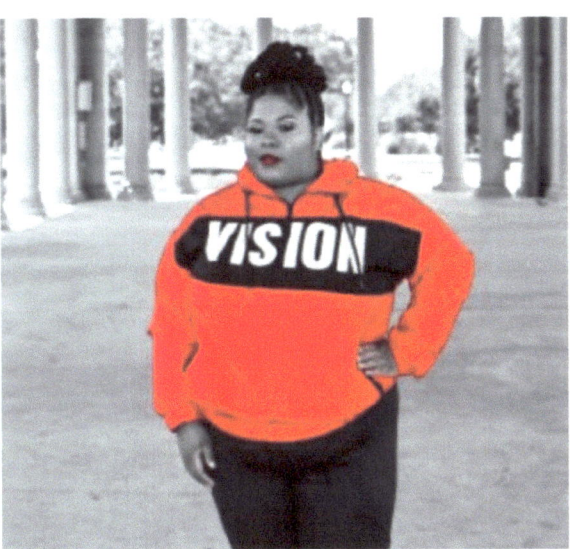

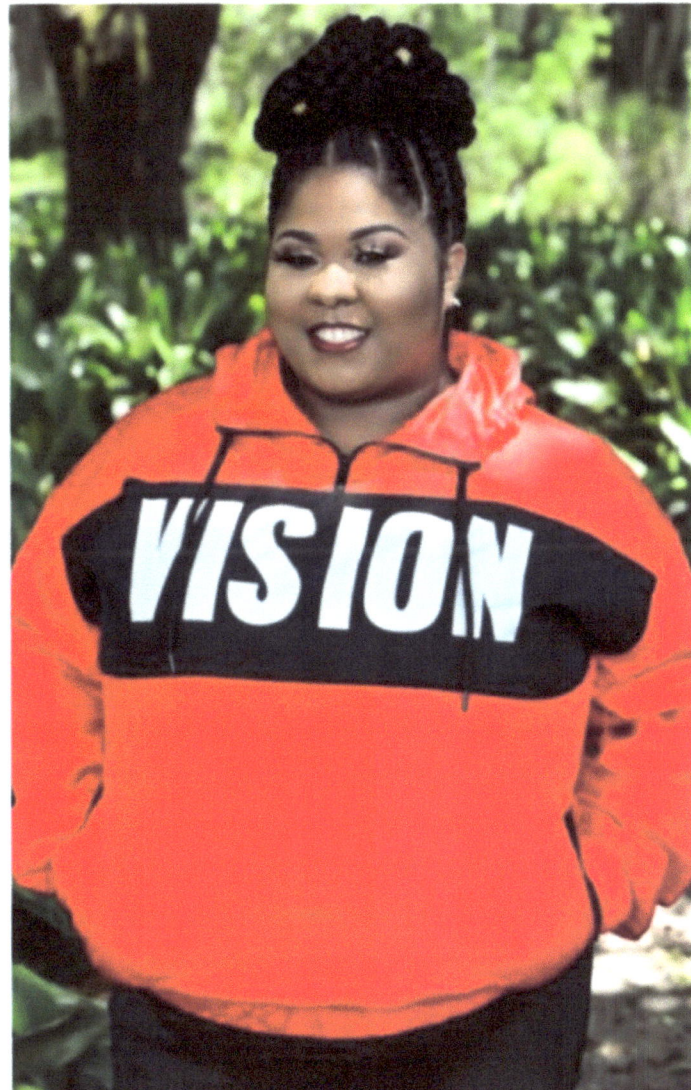

UNBOUNDED INTERNATIONAL
COURTNEY EVANS

Unbounded International Dance Theater is an up and coming dance company in New Orleans that specializes in Adult Dance Classes for women of all walks of life. These classes focus on the empowerment of women and cultivating a space where women are free to completely be themselves.

"Facebook: Unbounded International
Instagram: Unboundedint

B U N N I E
T H E
B L O G G E R

IG BunnieTheBlogger
FB Bunnie Mae
Twitter The Bunnie Hole

www.bunniehole.com

IMAGES : SEW6 PHOTOGRAPHY

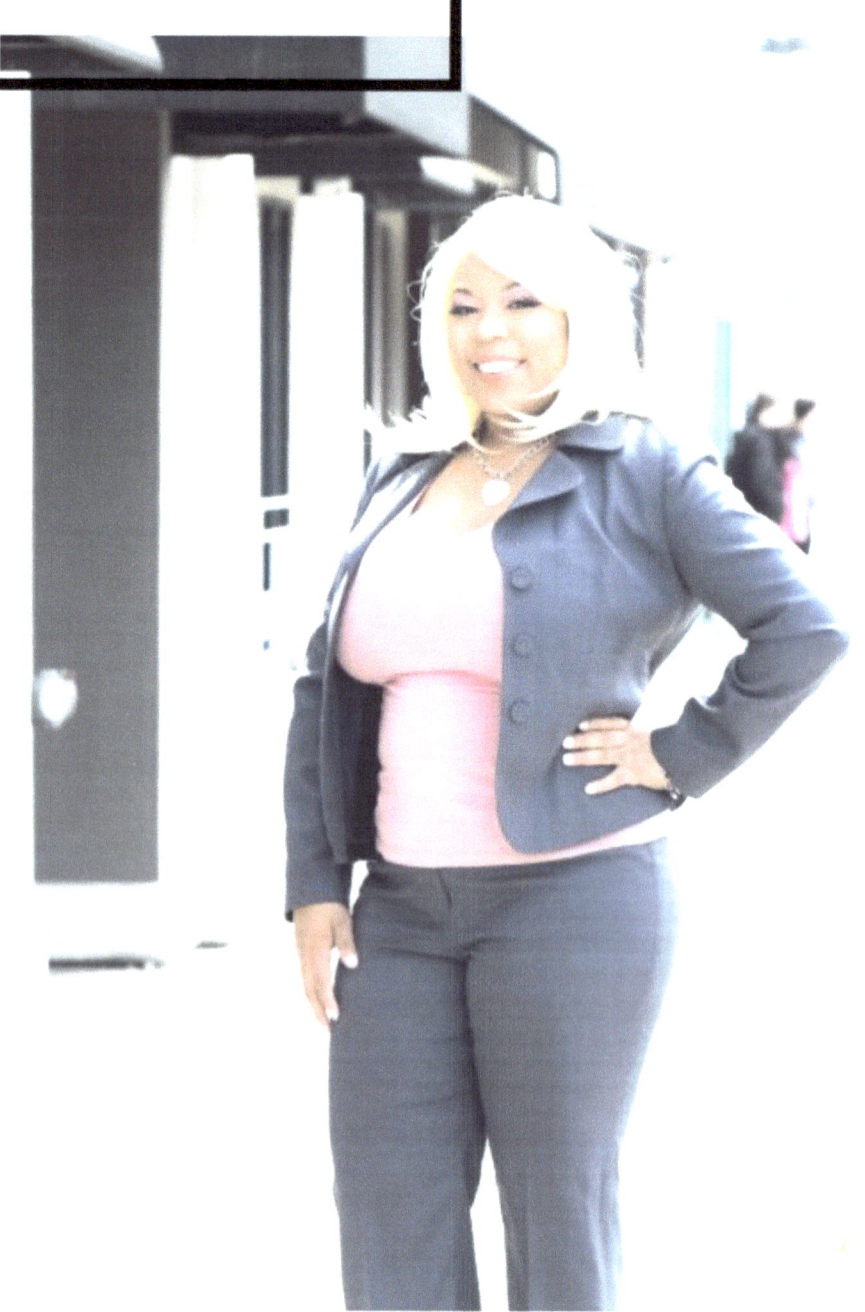

Bunnie is a Media Correspondent that has created her own lane as the Media Of the Midwest! Not only is she Motivational Speaker and Mindset Coach, Bunnie has forged her lane as a socialite and journalist. She has created a platform called The Bunnie Hole which is an inspirational and lifestyle platform for anyone looking to live their BEST life.Unapologetic and with No Limitations. The Bunnie Hole has quickly grown to a full media outlet! Bunnie has recently leveraged her career and created a platform called Girl Gang, which is a collective group of women pooled together to provide resources and sisterhood to women from all over the world! Bound to be a success, Bunnie is determined to not only create a successful lane for herself, but also for everyone around her!

Make sure you hop in and join Bunnie on the following platforms

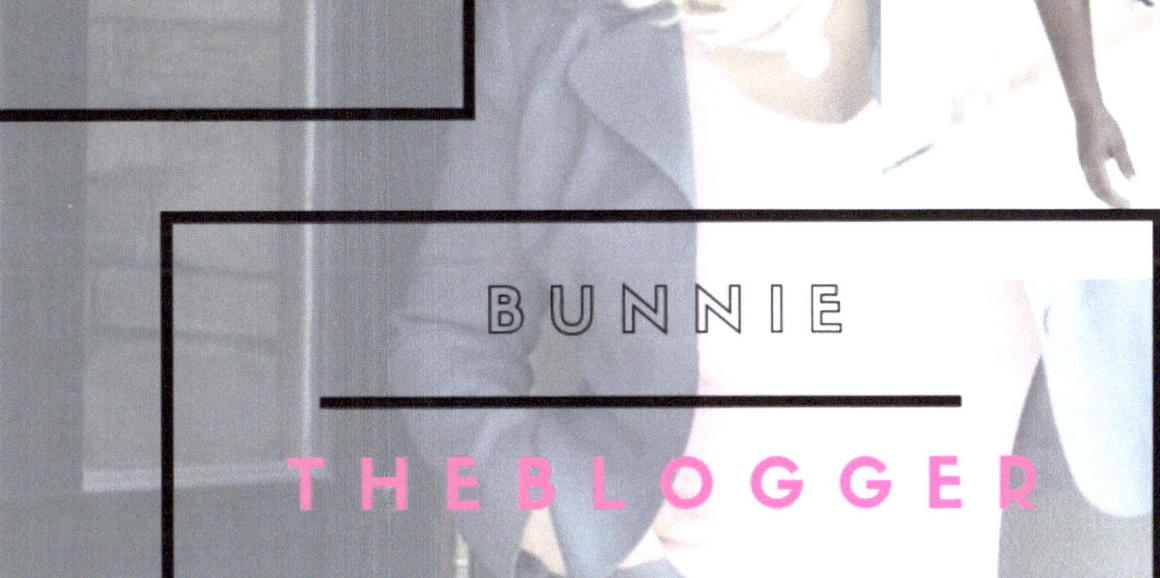

BUNNIE

THEBLOGGER

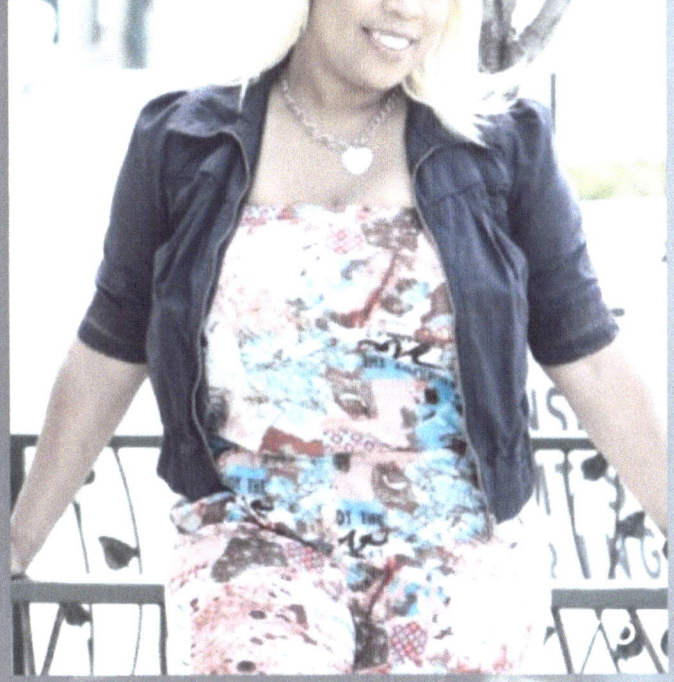

bunniehole.com

THE JOURNEY OF
JOI-LOUISE

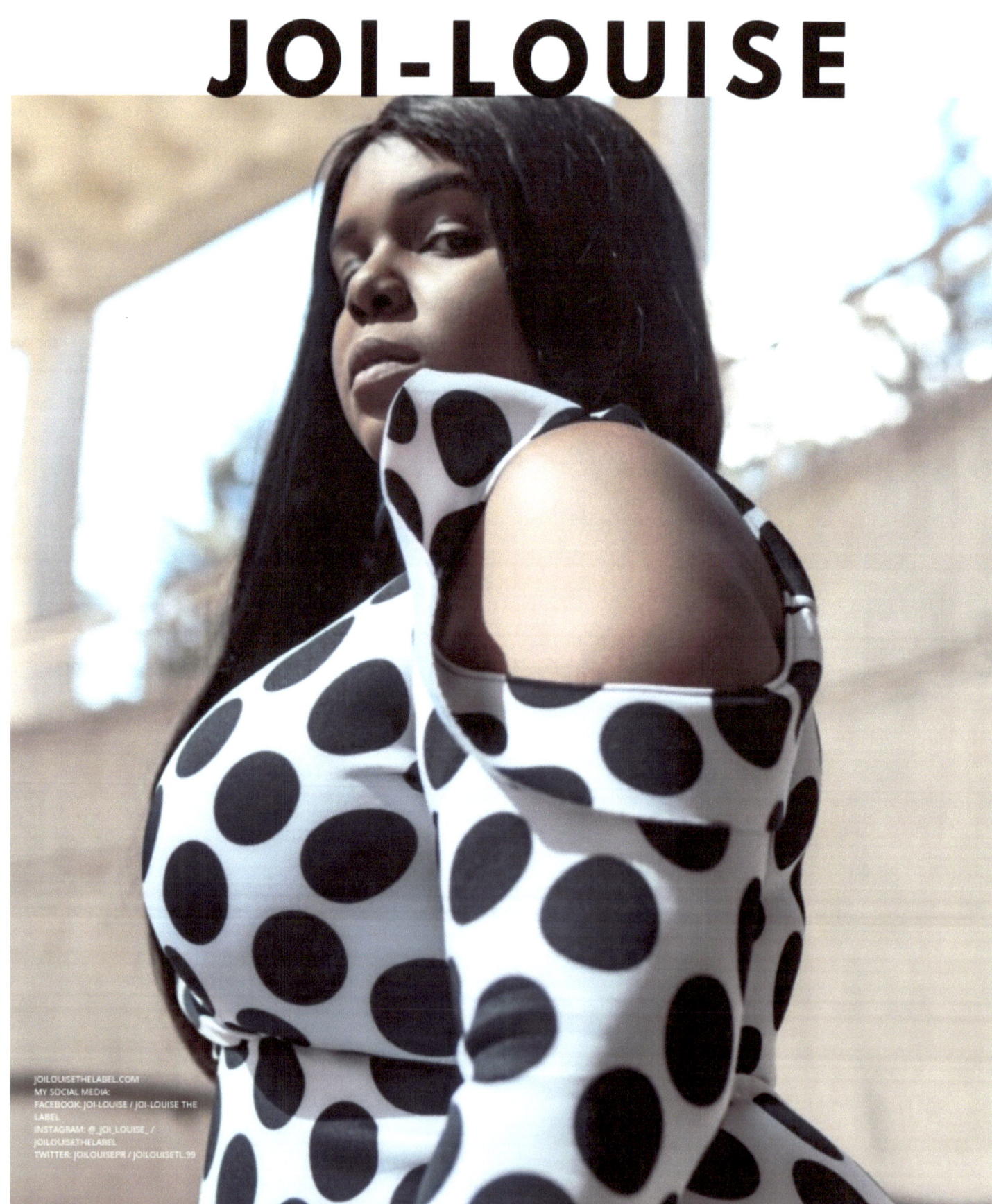

JOILOUISETHELABEL.COM
MY SOCIAL MEDIA:
FACEBOOK: JOI-LOUISE / JOI-LOUISE THE
LABEL
INSTAGRAM: @_JOI_LOUISE_ /
JOILOUISETHELABEL
TWITTER: JOILOUISEPR / JOILOUISETL_99

KEYS TO SUCCESS

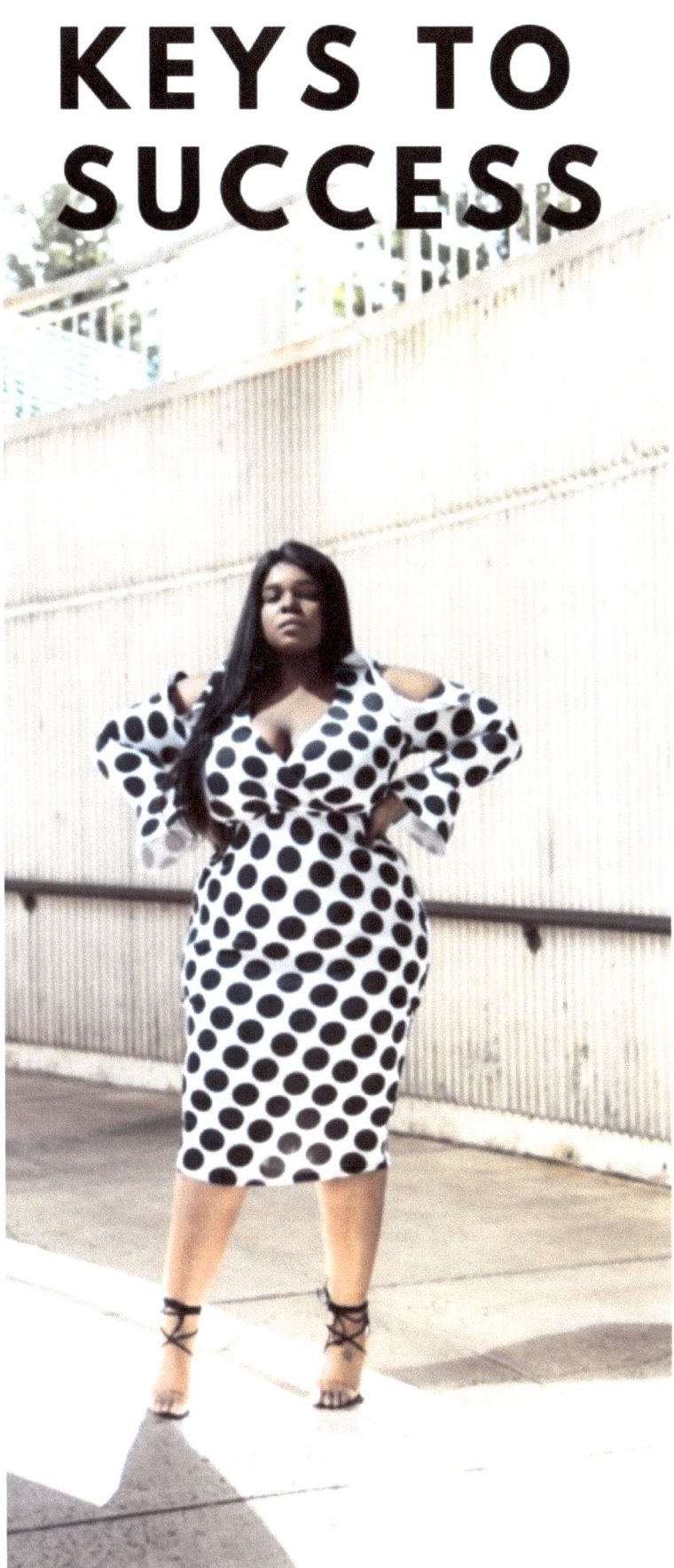

Joi-Louise Hall is the Creative Director of Joi-Louise The Label (JLTL). She holds a Fashion Design and Construction Degree from Wood Tobe-Coburn. JLTL was created on October of 2017 from the sheer desire for chic, premium printed apparel for women of all sizes.

Joi-Louise The Label is for women that are mad about prints, clean lines and chic style. The JLTL woman is not afraid to be seen. She dresses to make an impact with her style.

"Growing up, I was inspired by everyone from Fran Drescher in the Nanny and Glenn Close as Cruella de Ville in 101 Dalmatians to Olivia Newton-John in Grease...post makeover of course and Morticia Adams in the Adams Family."

"I hope my ladies feel stronger when they wear my designs. I hope they feel powerful and more than capable to take on ANYTHING that comes their way."

JUST START!

Many people think perfection is what will bring success and in thinking this they never start anything or see it through. When I started my first business back in 2012, I didn't care that I didn't know how to build a website nor did I care that I had never run an e-commerce store. I knew that I just needed to start. Fast-forward to today and I have learned so much since starting my first business. Although I have not achieved perfection, I am so much better because I took that leap. I build my own websites, set up my own Shopify store, create my own graphics and it all happened because I just started and learned everything I need to know along the way.

RESEARCH!

It is important to do your own research. It is an important part of the learning process as an entrepreneur. Teaching and learning are what will make you successful. When you're starting out, Google University will be your right hand. Don't let anyone tell you that Google is not a resource. It is how I taught myself to build a website, create a mailing list and how to run ads on Facebook for my businesses.

PLAN!

Get yourself a daily planner and really get organized and intentional about the things you want to achieve. Setting goals are one thing but mapping out how and when these goals will be achieved is what converts them into accomplishments. I wholeheartedly believe in vision boards. I created one at the top of the year that outlined things I wanted to accomplish such as my rebrand, press placements and entrepreneurial success for myself as a black female entrepreneur. I use my daily planner to make sure that I break those macro goals into micro goals and intentionally act on making them accomplishments. It's important that you do this because it makes the goals less overwhelming. When you are building a business on your own it's very easy to become overwhelmed and lose momentum on achieving your goals.

BUILD A NETWORK!

You cannot do this alone. I am able to work independently but I very much prefer to work in a team. Two heads are indeed better than one. I have cultivated relationships with so many people that have supported me in getting to where my brand is today. I have built a network with everyone from bloggers, photographers, makeup artists, and other female entrepreneurs. You are only as strong as your network. Get out there and genuinely connect with people that will make you stronger. I remember needing help taking ghost mannequin photos of my Tribal Print Dress back in 2017. The turnaround time to get these photos submitted for a once in a lifetime opportunity for my brand was less than 24 hours. If I hadn't had connections with a photographer that had his own studio, who knows if I would have been able to eat the photos done. Your network is EVERYTHING!

NEVER GIVE UP!

Success doesn't happen overnight. It takes self development, discipline, and resourcefulness. I started my first business seven years ago and with each day I just get better and better. Even when things seem slow or stagnant, it only means you need to reevaluate things and try them with a different angle or perspective. I wouldn't have created what I have today if I gave up on myself years ago. Success takes persistence and tenacity.

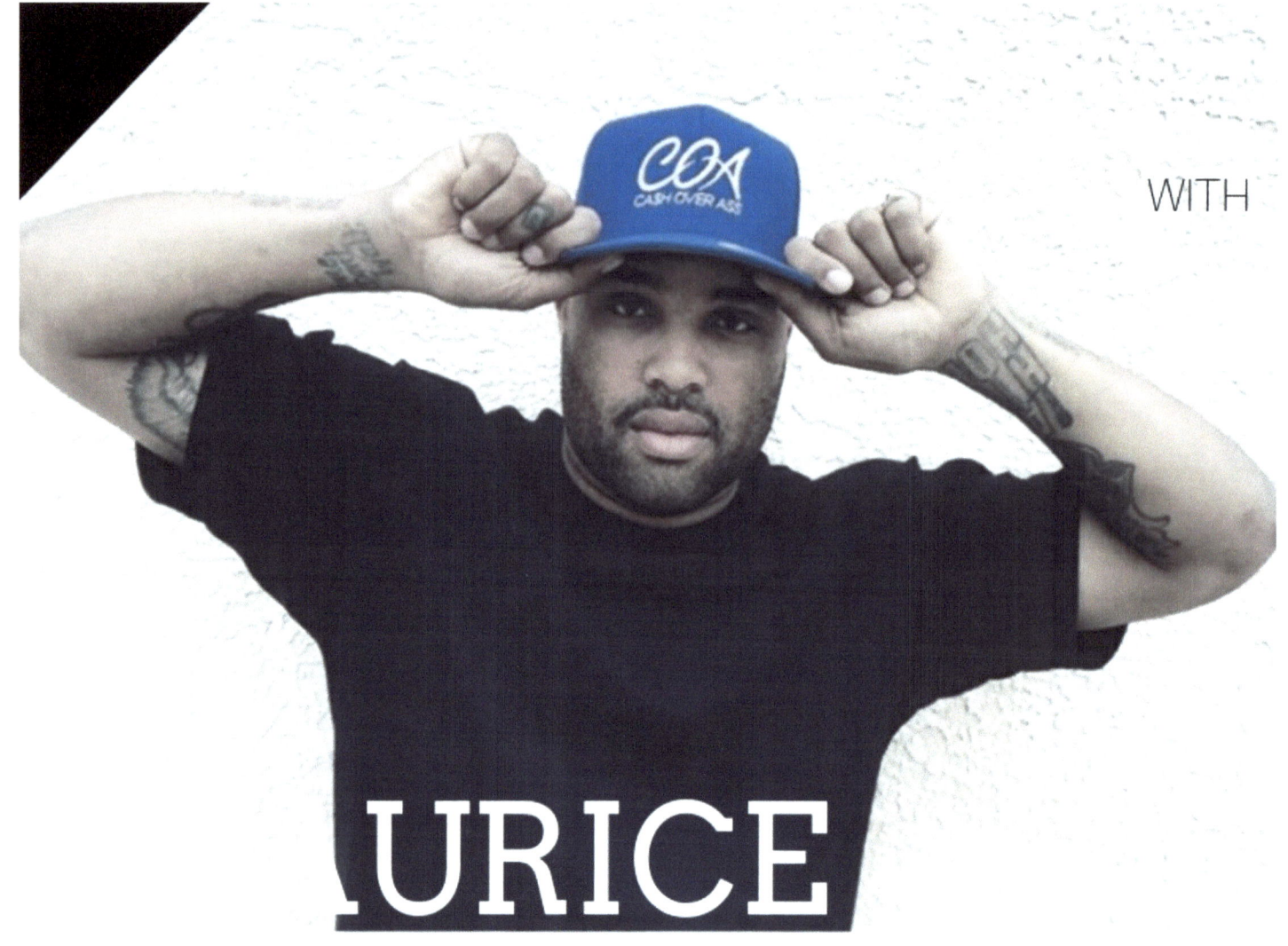

WITH

URICE
BELISLE

WRITTEN BY LISA LOPEZ

I was inspired by 2PAC M.O.B when I created my brand C.O.A. in 2017. I wanted to do something a little different in the urban fashion community . C.O.A is a reminder that it's all about securing the bag first.

As a local rap artist in South Central Los Angeles I wanted to create a brand that let everyone know let's stay focus on getting the CASH.

I'M GETTING TIRED AND, FRANKLY, IT'S ABOUT TIME I TALK ABOUT IT.

BEHIND THE
SCENE

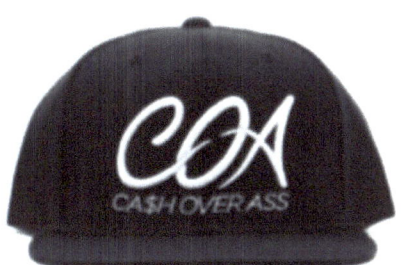
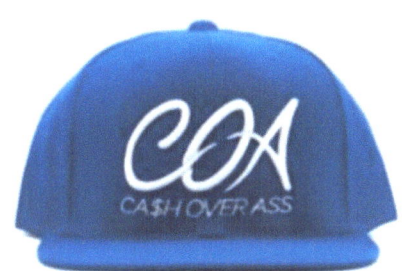

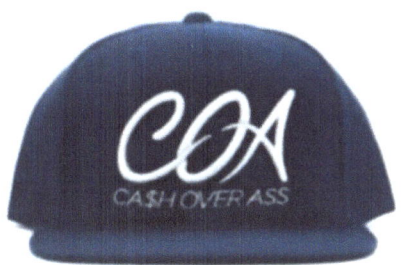
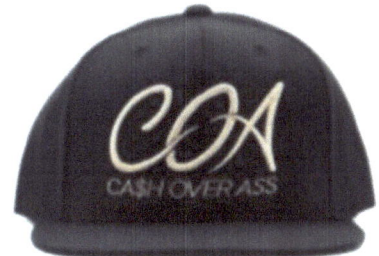

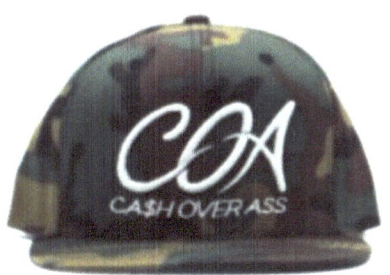
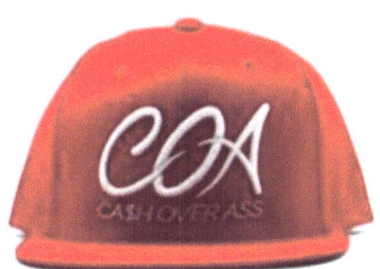

C.O.A

BRAND CREATED BY MAURICE BELISLE ALSO
KNOWN AS RAP ARTIST FLYDAUNO

SOCIAL MEDIA HANDLES
IG:@CASHOVERASS2017
FACEBOOK @CASHOVERASS2017S

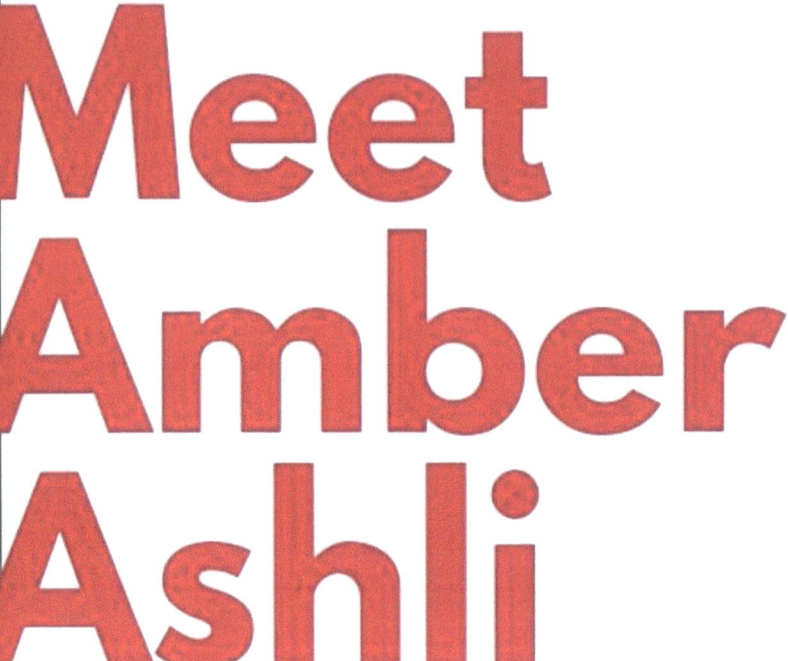

Meet Amber Ashli

ISTMSTYLESTM was launched February 14th, 2017. The brand represents individuality and speaks to those who are unapologetically fearless to be themselves, while being fly. It is a unisex brand that meshes the tomboy aesthetic with prominent taboo attitude.

The collections are available every odd year starting from the launch date for a duration of six months. It is exclusively isochronous because the drop months will always be February to June with July being a giveaway month. The product is only available for that month duration. Our first product was the "Ring Thee Alarm" Strapback that dropped February 14, 2017 until March 14, 2017. In July, we randomly choose ten Instagram followers to receive one mystery gift.

The Brand
An independent published fashion stylist, clothing curator and art enthusiast, born in Manhattan, New York. Amber Ashli loves fashion and to make people feel comfortable in whatever they wear.
What does ISTMSTYLES™ mean? At the age of 19, she developed the acronym I.S.T.M. Ask her what each letter represents when you work with her so a conversation can be had. STYLES was added to complete the name, plus it's what she does so it fits!
She is the first African-American female student to graduate with a Bachelors of Science in Civil Engineering from Central CT State University.

"Your New favorite stylist taking on the big city."

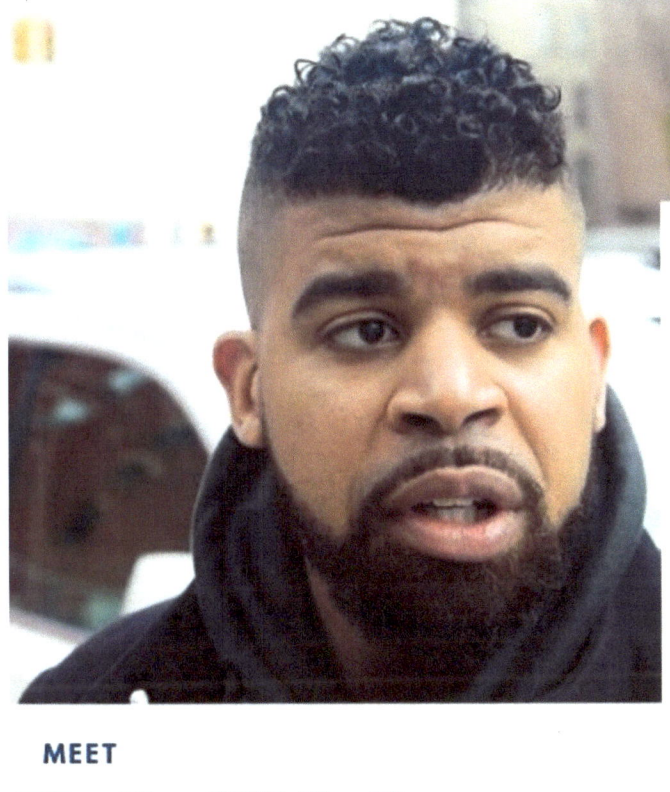

MEET

BLEU PABLO

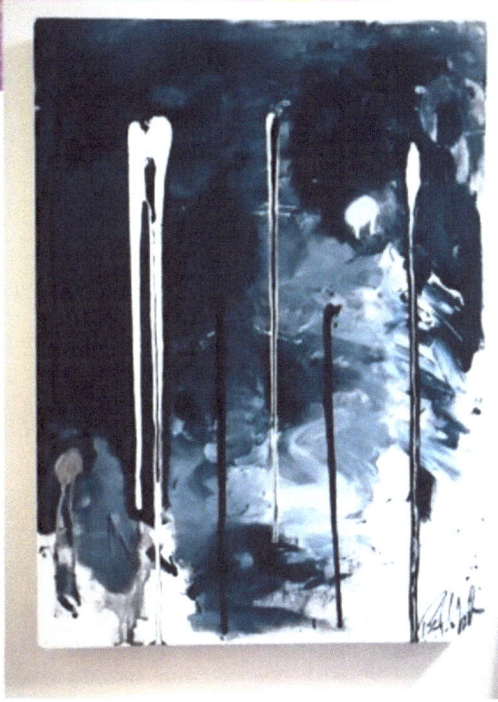

MManaging Director of The NYC Art Collective "Bleucalf": Elijah Wrighton also know as "Bleu Pablo" was born in The Bronx, NY 1991. Coming from a family of creatives, Bleu discovered his passion for painting through the work of his Great Uncle Albert Wright. His love for people fuels his motivation to create. "I'm inspired by human emotion, through textures and bold colors I want to be able take the subject out of his or her reality to evolve feelings of love, passion, and despair", says Bleu.

—

His ultimate goal is to continue to create and work with other platforms to give artist in inner city's more opportunities to showcase their work. Bleu has been featured on Experience Magazine, Huffington Post, Canvii and many more.

The NYC Art Collective "Bleucalf"

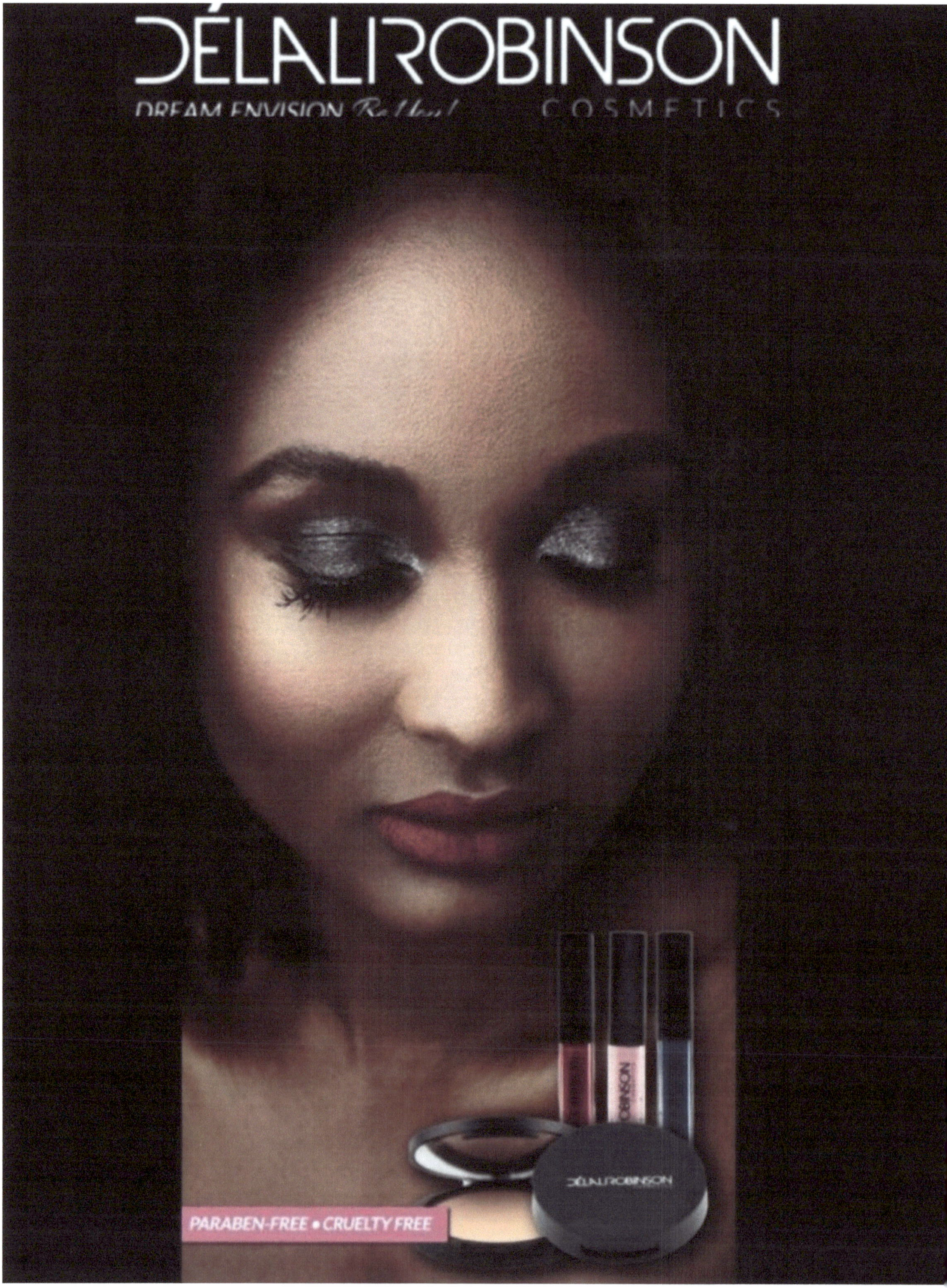
DÉLALIROBINSON
DREAM ENVISION
COSMETICS
PARABEN-FREE • CRUELTY FREE

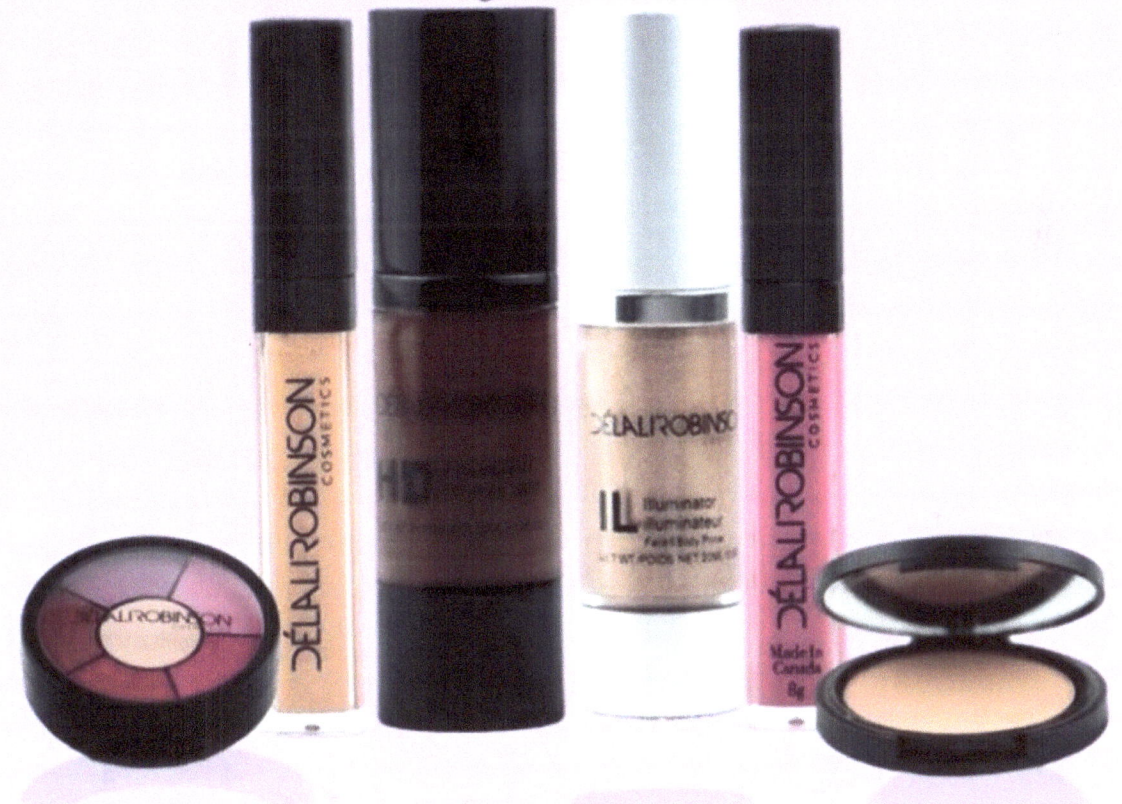

THE FASHION FAMILY OF INSTAGRAM

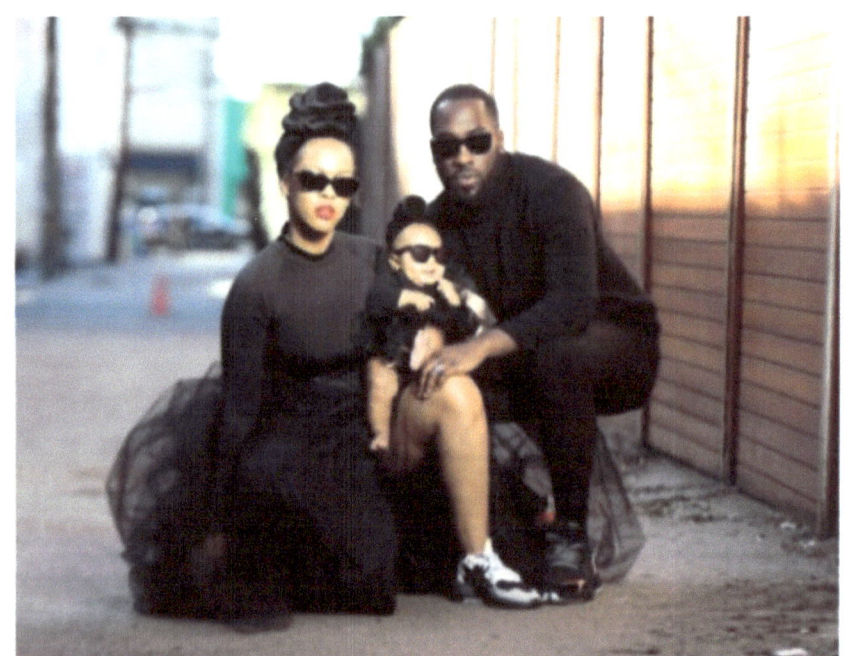

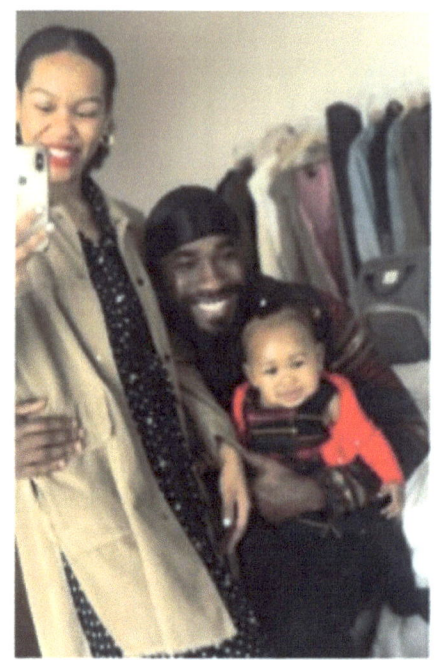

FAMILY FIRST

Victor was born and raised in Newark, NJ. With his interest in music, fashion, travel, and food, Victor Okunzuwa Osawe started to present his sense of style to his audience in early 2015. He has secured successful collaborations with some industry's most respected tastemakers, including Members Only, Original Penguin, GQ, Ugg, Fila, Reebok, BoohooMan, Express, and Daniel Wellington. Victor Okunzuwa Osawe is currently based in Los Angeles, California.

SOCIAL MEDIA

Victor Okunzuwa Osawe
Social Media Influencer/ Personal Wardrobe Stylist

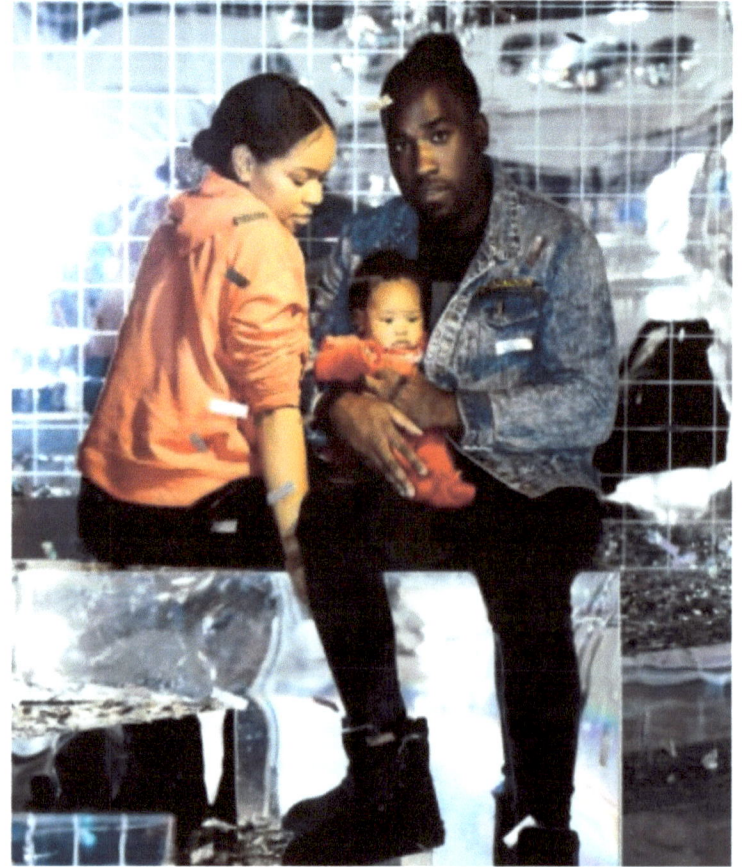

FunknCrystals

Are unique Eyewear brand that utilizes natural
gemstones and healing crystals to create
eyewear that vibrates higher.

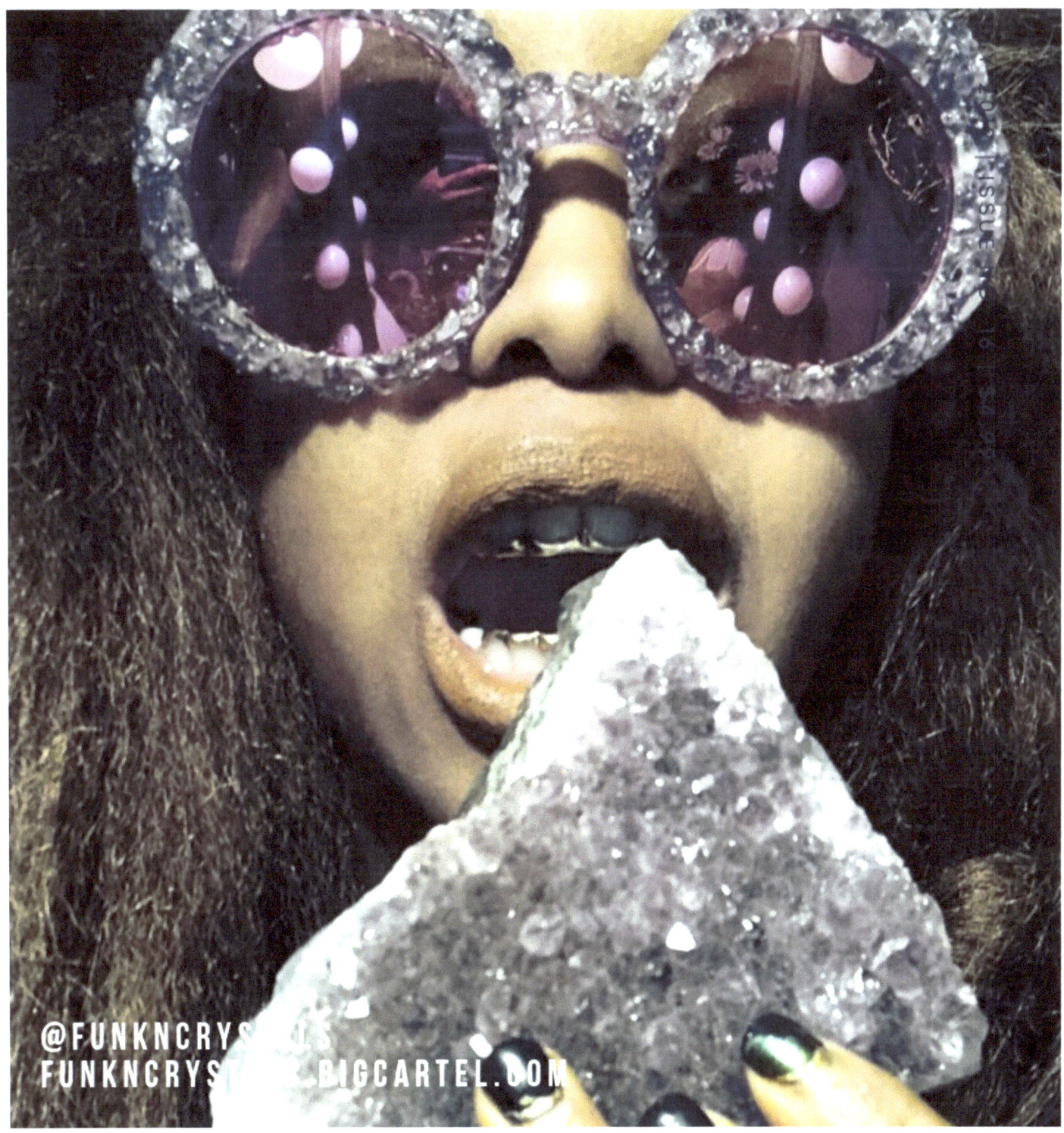

@FUNKNCRYSTALS
FUNKNCRYSTALS.BIGCARTEL.COM

www.ingramcontent.com/pod-product-compliance
Lightning Source LLC
Chambersburg PA
CBHW051108180526
45172CB00002B/821